SALOONS

OF

(OLD & NEW)

NEVADA

"Whiskey and Ditch" also sometimes called "Booze and Branch" or "Bourbon and Water" – but whatever the call, this book recounts some of the history and anecdotes concerning drinking... in "old Nevada" saloons.

Drinking has been a Nevada tradition since the inception of the state. Over the years a certain custom and etiquette has evolved which has elevated merely tippling to a high art. Saloons were the vehicle of this transformation. Below is a very typical saloon interior in early Nevada. The location and date are unknown. Note the man in the center who is "pouring his own" – an old Nevada custom which has now died out.

Photo: Nevada Historical Society.

DEDICATION

They were exciting, vibrant times. A new society was being formed in a new world and under the most trying conditions. This new population was mainly young, virile, single men; all far from home and customary inhibitions, subject to continuous hazards and unable to escape their immediate desolate environment. It was a rugged situation inevitably leading to the wild forms of solace and release they so eagerly desired.

And thus it was natural that the town saloon— or saloons—as was more often the case—became the centers for this "source of release". The early saloon was the hub of business and community life; it was the gathering place for all segments of the population since it constituted an arena where all were equal; it was the focus of most social interactions and probably the warmest place in town.

The modern "bar", in large and busy casinos, is the very antithesis of the old traditional Nevada saloon. It does not operate as, or even pretend to be, a convivial gathering place and focus of community relations and communication, but is rather only an adjunct to the more important aspect of serious gaming. Drinks are often "comped" to active and heavy players by skimpily clad waitresses; there is no finesse, no relaxation, nothing that would relate to the earlier era of real saloon intimacy. Bartenders are often disinterested, on straight shifts and everyone seems to be only going through the motions. There is no confidence, no talk, no socializing. Drinking has been reduced to a cold, dirty business with the "bottom line" as the only concern.

But the traditional Nevada saloon attitude does exist in some smaller independent bars, particularly "neighborhood bars" where patronage is steady and "everyone knows your name"[1] and especially in the smaller more remote locations, the rural towns and crossroads that still manage to exist in the Nevada outback. There the old Nevada saloon can still be found in all its original glory. It is to all these establishments that this book is dedicated.

There are a number of bars throughout the state which are not to be found in this review. These were omitted because in my view, and solely in my view, they do not meet the parameters of Old Nevada Saloons and therefore do not qualify. No disrespect is intended in any case.

…and there may be a few left out that do qualify. To these I extend my sincere apologies.

---

1) As they do in "Cheers" - that famous Boston Pub.

CREDITS

Marcia Elliot - Deputy County Clerk County - Eureka County

Rita Phillips & others at the Nevada Historical Society, Reno.

Marshall Fey - Liberty Belle Saloon - Reno

Carlos Morales - Sundance Casino, Winnemucca

Howard Hickson & North Eastern Nevada Museum, Elko

Pansie Lee Larson - Humboldt County Museum, Winnemucca

Gage Smith, Scott Smith, Bret Duster, Jerry Mock and Jim Lawrence – Photographs

Luana Martin, Cheryl Powers & others - Typing

G.W. Gus Keller - early resident of Vernon. (Nevada State Journal, 1958).

Carson Valley Historical Society

Douglas County Library

Nevada State Library

Nevada State Museum

Frankovich Family (pictures of Winehouse, Reno)

Irene Scott - Winnemucca (photos of Gem Bar – Winnemucca)

Record-Courier Newspaper – Gardnerville

All maps by Jack Moore.

Books:

The Town that Died Laughing – Oscar Lewis

Comstock Mining and Miners – Elliot Lord

A Peep at Washoe – J. Ross Browne

Northeast Nevada Frontier – Patterson, Ulph & Goodwin

Goldfield – Hugh Shamberger

History of Tonopah – Robert McCracken

Copper Times – Jack Fleming

Pioneers of the Ponderosa – Myers Sauer Ratay.

Nevada Ghost Towns and Mining Camps – S. W. Paher

A special recognition is given to "This Was Nevada" series #90, #201, #202, & #238, by Phillip I. Earl (Nevada Historical Society) which appeared in the Nevada State Journal in January 1977, March 1979 and November 1979.

TABLE OF CONTENTS

Chandelier – <u>The Crystal</u> (Saloon) in Virginia City.

INTRODUCTION

It is difficult to visualize the frenetic activity that characterized the early day Nevada mining camp. Life in those times was "vivid" to say the least.

An illuminating account is contained in an article by Albert S. Evans which appeared in the *Overland Monthly* magazine of March 1865. The town described was Hamilton[1], but it could have been many others:

Bullwhackers and Jezebels

"Across the wide, treeless mirage valley, over the low pancake mountain, across another and narrower valley, and we enter at last the long winding canyon which leads up to the White Pine Mountain Range which terminates at Hamilton...long lines of mules and oxen drawing heavy wagons laden with supplies of every kind...mill machinery, whiskey, mule feed and whiskey again. Jerkwater stages which had been three or four days making the trip of 110 miles to Hamilton with passengers for the mines; mine owners, or those who had but recently sold mines and were "flush" on horseback, bull wackers in soldiers' coats, with whips a dozen feet in length on poles longer still, just in from Austin or Wadsworth; honest miners with salted claims ready to sell to the newly arrived greenhorns; foot packers without a cent who had packed their blankets and luggage all the way from Elko...painted jezebels from every mining camp from Idaho to Sonora; Shoshone Indians, Chinamen and capitalists who, in San Francisco were ever known as men with plethoric bank accounts...(all) crowded the streets of Hamilton. All was bustle and hurry, noise, excitement and confusion. The stores and saloons were crowded with men in huge overcoats, the pockets of which were filled with rock specimens of varying value. The many bidders expended frenetic efforts to supply the demand for drinks which poured in from every direction." It is this "demand for drinks" that still interests us down to this modern day.

Unfortunately very few photographs of early day Hamilton exist. However some of the later boom towns, such as Goldfield, for instance, which where part of the 1906 period were much better captured on film and thus preserved for an understanding of what it must have been like. On the next page is a typical street scene of that town in 1905. Notice the row of saloons, the dance halls, the mud streets, and the freighting activity. Hamilton was quite similar.

---

1) Hamilton was without doubt one of the more important early day Nevada towns, at one time even threatening Virginia City for dominance. It was located in White Pine County, about 21 miles westerly of Ely, a few miles south of present U. S. 50 and is now within the Nevada National Forest area. Hamilton became a large city, certainly by Nevada standards. At its height it boasted 30,000 people, supported by over 100 saloons (and 23 lawyers). The town boomed rapidly from its inception in 1868; only 24 months later, by 1870, there were 13,000 recorded mining claims and over 25,000 people had stampeded to the region, often abandoning established claims in "less promising" sites. A city of tents and huts, rock windbreaks and caves sprang up; but it did not last and it is (virtually) totally gone today. My grandfather, then a young immigrant from Switzerland, kept store in Hamilton in 1885.

Goldfield 1906. Photo: Courtesy of the Nevada Historical Society.

What was left of Hamilton about 1963. Photo: *Nevada Highways* magazine.

ONE

THE OLD NEVADA SALOON

Saloons in Nevada have always played an important part in the developing society. This was particularly so in the earlier mining period when the saloon was usually the first commercial operation in camp and was always the gathering place or center of town by common consent, whatever its origins. The first saloons where usually crude affairs and often served a multiple purpose as bar, hotel, general store, restaurant, post office and barber, since no other places as yet existed to supply these services. The bar itself was often just a plank over two kegs or sometimes a sluice box, or a wagon gate, or whatever was handy. But its role as the entertainment and social core was undisputed. While the "better" element in town may have looked down upon such places, they were usually few in number and therefore of little consequence . The isolation, loneliness and hardships of the early remote desert camps also soon made the saloons a social and psychological requirement. The drudgery and danger of working far underground, sometimes in boiling hot water, with rotten timbering and ever present dangers of explosives and cave-ins could be momentarily forgotten over a few belts of "rotgut" or "bluenose", and the warm interiors of the buildings offered a very welcome escape from a rock cave cut into the hillside or a wood frame boarding house where the cold northerly winds "blew right through. "

The liquor served over the "Plank" was sometimes potent enough to kill, but matched the character of their existence. Generally it was nothing more than cheap alcohol mixed with anything handy, This might include burnt sugar (for color), cheap rum, various flavorings, tobacco or whatever . The names of the various liquors dispersed were equally colorful. A well known drink, for example, was "Shawn O'Farrell", a glass of whiskey with a beer chaser (still in vogue in various places). "Whiskey was to cut the dust and the beer to quench the thirst", but it was sometimes claimed that the beer was necessary to wash the whiskey down before the drinker choked to death. Others were Taos Lightening, Forty Rod, Red Eye, Rattlesnake Juice, Hemlock Brandy, White Mule and Panther Piss. Colloquial names were much in vogue. A bartender could be asked for: Pinetop, Popskull, Shepherd's Delight, Stagger Soup, Nose Paint, Coffin Varnish, Valley Tan, Blue Ruin, Tiger Spit, Tangleleg, Red Dynamite, Nockum Stiff, Bugjuice, & Miner's Friend.

Then, and now, a Nevadan who did not drink was considered somewhat strange since a friendly glass was a sort of handshake between men on equal terms. It was also a panacea for high expectations or to offset disappointments. It is said that in the early Nevada camps, about one-fifth of the saloon patrons were celebrating their good luck; the remaining four-fifths were despondent because they had not been so lucky, at least not as yet.

A strong custom and an accepted etiquette regarding drinking soon developed. Whiskey was sold to all customers at the same price (generally "two bits"[1]) with the third or fourth drink uniformly "on the house."

---

1) "Two bits" is 25 cents, in the vernacular of the old west. Drinks at most better saloons were two bits; it was a sad day indeed, accompanied by distraught public mourning when a saloon in Gold Hill, just over the divide from Virginia City, found it necessary to lower prices to become "one bit" houses. This was due to declining volumes of ore, but it was the "handwriting on the wall" and everyone knew it!

In some camps the bartender set up the first drink free (when the miners came off shift) and sometimes the first drink in the morning was also free. Occasionally this custom was abused with some (more thirsty) patrons visiting 12 or 13 saloons before breakfast, but usually this was limited, perhaps to only six or seven places.

Then, and now, it was not acceptable to drink "alone." If a person wished solitude he was left alone but common custom required that he first offer to buy the barkeep a drink, or if he accepted a drink from a fellow patron, he was expected to buy a round of drinks to reciprocate. If he did not have the funds to do so, he was to indicate that fact before he accepted the drink. And, if he was lucky at the gaming tables, he was expected to buy drinks for the rest of the crowd. (This is still the custom in some of the smaller rural establishments).

Sometimes the main feature of the saloon, especially if the establishment had prospered from its earlier years, was life-sized painting of a (very) nubile girl positioned just above eye level at the back bar. Most of these were totally naked, but sometimes they were "coyly involved with a fan" or possible suitably and subtly camouflaged by a palm leaf or something.[2] Other improvements followed. Curtains were installed over windows, rugs replaced plain pine floors and sometimes fancy chandeliers provided light and atmosphere. During this period the typical western long bar evolved, as did chairs arranged around the round heating stove and the gambling array lined along the opposite wall. The bar also became more ornate, featuring hand rubbed exotic woods and turned columns. Some of these were truly masterpieces of cabinetry, especially those in the larger communities, such as Virginia City, Tonopah or Gold Hill, but the best were the "Brunswick Bars", imported from England. The saloon itself was personified by the people who worked there, especially the barkeep. In the earliest days of a new camp, the bartender was usually as disreputable as was his customers. Hair, dirt and toughness were the order of the day and the host had to be "one of the boys." Later as the profits increased, he could and did afford better. With money the barkeep (also the banker, lawyer and politician) became more respectable. He manicured his beard, trimmed the shoulder length hair, acquired a new suit complete with a colorful vest and a watch chain and thus attained an overnight respectability sufficient in some cases to be elected Mayor, Marshall or even Judge.[3] Whatever their appearance, most barkeeps were known for their good cheer and general humor. They were also the camps social psychologists, bankers (sometimes even extending credit), and often provided a warm night's bed (on the floor) for those in need. Many served as the local news director, umpired disagreements and performed as marriage counselors or just listened.[4]

---

2) "Those hungry and thirsty souls who flock daily into the neat, cool and genteel establishment of Goodman and McClusky on Main Street have surely often cast a glance on the large painting hanging in rather poor light. This picture, represents a reclining Venus being crowned by cupid, at whose feet sit a lovesick troubadour with a mandolin. It is a copy of the original by Guido Reni hanging in the Royal Gallery in Dresden Germany. Three bullet holes in various parts of the body somewhat reduces the overall value but considerably enhances, in some strange way, it appeal." White Pine News 1869, It was, as might be imagined, just slightly lurid.

3) Mark Twain once wrote, "The cheapest and easiest way to become an influential man and be looked up to by the community at large was to stand behind a bar, wear a cluster diamond pin and sell whiskey."

4) These attitudes and customs, too, have been (somewhat) passed down through the years and there are a few modern local saloons which still perform some of these same informal services.

To refuse a drink from a stranger was a most serious violation of saloon etiquette. A refusal without an adequate explanation was taken as a direct and unforgivable insult. There was more than one killing as a result of this particular form of bar etiquette. A typical example occurred on 24 February, 1877, in Elko, when Larry Lynch entered the Idaho Saloon and "called a number of persons up to drink"–one of whom was a man named Hubbard. Hubbard offhandedly declined whereupon Lynch called him an S.O.B. Hubbard started to walk away however, and Lynch then "pummeled" him, an act which soon deteriorated into a fully blown first fight and eventually a gun battle. Lynch died in the affair from a blow to the head.

Bartending could also be quite dangerous. Such was the case in Tonopah in 1901. A Frank McAllister, already "three sheets to the wind," staggered into the Mizpah and asked for a drink, which was refused by the barkeep who advised him that he had already had enough. McAllister left, but returned a half hour later and staggered over to where the night bartender was relaxing before the potbellied stove. The drunk whipped out his gun, threatened to "perforate his carcass" if he did not "instanter" get back behind the bar and pour him a drink. Under this duress there was little argument. The barkeep headed for the bar, but he kept both eyes on the now weaving and wobbling gunman. Seeing his chance, the barman whirled, stepped sideways, grabbed the gun and smashed the drunk once over the head with the butt. He hit him again as he started to rise and finally McAllister crawled to the door and staggered into the night. The local newspaper editorialized indignantly "if the time has come when a bartender in this town has to look down a cocked gun every time he sees fit to refuse a drunken man a drink, it is time a halt is called."

In Bodie one night the bartender and a customer consummated an argument by firing at each other point blank across the bar. The first to go was the mirror (a favorite target which could hardly be missed) and then a barrel of cider which was plugged and began to spurt all over the room. At this point, a gambler entered from an adjacent gaming parlor and had his cigar shot out of his mouth. Thinking he was the target, the gambler drew his gun and joined the fusillade. Fifteen shots were fired, but only one person was hit and that was minor.

Their clientele reflected the entire camp; everyone frequented the various saloons of the town.[5] Even the preacher would use a saloon to deliver impromptu services prior to the erection of a church (one pioneer Nevadan remembers the first establishment in town was a saloon set up in a tent.) Soon there were ten girls from who knows where. Then a piano forte was brought over the mountains on mule back at great trouble and expense. There were 12 such establishments flourishing before the preacher got his little church going. That is not to say, however, that everyone was devoted to drinking. In some towns there were various vigilante groups dedicated to preserving the peace and that usually meant limiting drinking somehow. These groups were not too successful in the early camps, but as they matured and more women became permanent residents, their efforts and influence was more pronounced.

---

5) In Canderleria during the 1880's, there were twenty-seven saloons before there was a church. Pioche, in 1871, had 85 saloons in a town of only about 7,000 people.

The saloons also provided many of the amusements in the camp. All saloons boasted gaming tables and gaming ran a close second to drinking. Dancing was also common, even if the miners had to dance with one another. Prostitution, as might be expected, was also prevalent. Drama and theatrics were popular occasions in early Nevada and saloons often served as impromptu theaters. The saloon could (and did) also serve, on occasions, as a funeral parlor, operating table or political arena. The saloon was also frequently the stage station. Water was scarce and barely fit for drinking anyway; the weather was usually either too hot or too cold to remain outside, but pleasant enough inside so that anyone even the most prim eastern lady could sit at a table while horses were being changed and eventually everyone became accustomed to the constant noise, the naked painting, the smell of cheap whiskey, unwashed bodies and the general tawdriness of the scene. It was part of the west. And those who had been successful and could now afford the finest clothes, smoke the best cigars and drink the finest liquor seldom forgot their more humble beginnings and all classes mingled without the slightest hint of any social distinction.

The saloon then was the real core of the mining camp, a buffer and a refuge from the problems and turmoil of the day. And it still is, especially in the rural areas of Nevada. The local saloon still exerts a strong influence and is the social cynosure of large areas otherwise devoted to sagebrush, coyotes and nothingness. It is a gathering place, a place to meet your friends and to make new ones; it is a warm refuge in a cold world and a cool haven during hot summer afternoons. It is the common consent center of a vast tributary area, a place in which celebrations are held, community hijinks perpetuated and local color established or embellished. Many a Nevada town would not be a "place" without it's own particular and unique watering hole.

Of all the Nevada towns where life revolved around their saloons, Virginia City, the "Queen of the Comstock", was the most outstanding. In fact, Virginia City's first business premises, located in 1859 at the corner of B and Sutton Streets, was a "tent saloon" of one Charlie Sturm, whose establishment, the Express Bar Room, was to be model of hundreds that followed.[6] Slightly later, Sturm and Wells Fargo agent, Dave Ward, after experiencing a leaking (canvas) roof one afternoon following a rare rainstorm and being duly concerned that such unwarranted water might potentially dilute their potions, erected the first brick structure in town, which became both the Express Bar Room and the Wells Fargo office for several years.

From earliest days saloons meant "relaxation." Relaxation usually meant booze, gambling, girls, frolic and fight, but not necessarily in that order. All of these were in demand and generally in high supply every night, but especially on Saturday night, in every one of the multitudinous Virginia City saloons. Even as early as 1866 there were 70 licensed saloons in the town, plus 15 more in Gold Hill.[7] But every hotel, restaurant, grocery store and even candy shops also sold liquor. At its heyday every fourth door on C Street was a licensed liquor dispensing establishment. These ranged from scores of "blind pigs" (simple speakeasies) to the best, such as the Crystal Bar "where gentlemen meet."

---

6)   In many of the smaller outlying camps the tent saloon was quite common. Tents, in fact, were the only structures in town. The operation at Gold Reef in 1907 is a prime example. See page 15.

7)   Wells Drury, famous Virginia City newspaper reporter, reported that in 1867 there were 100 saloons in Virginia City, 37 more in Gold Hill and seven in Silver City, a total of 144 plus 10 wholesale outlets and five breweries.

In between were the hangdog bars where whiskey mixed with "shudders" were served. And, in every saloon some kind of gambling prevailed; faro, rondo, roulette, red and black, chukaluck and dice were common. From about 1862 to the peak years of 1875 the average daily wage for some 15,000 miners in the diggings was $4/day or $120/month. Since living costs averaged at $50/month, this left the rest to "feed the tiger"[8] or to imbibe "tarantula" juice, often in equal amounts and sometimes with equally disastrous results.

From the earliest time drinking was the obsession of this town. On the Comstock it was estimated that consumption averaged a quart of whiskey per day per person—a drink at a time. Drinks cost 12 1/2 cents (one-bit) in the more ordinary establishments but increased to "two bits" (25 cents) in the more elaborate places such as those with an ornate mahogany bar and a large mirror. Strangely, there were very few drunkards. This is attributed to the common practice of drinking "glass by glass" which tended to inhibit immediate and overwhelming intoxication.

Saloon interior Tonopah 1905. The women at the center table legally couldn't be there until 1906.
Photo: Nevada Historical Society.

Wells Drury once wrote, "I recall when an ornery stranger reeled into a C Street saloon and pounding the bar with a six shooter until the glasses danced, announced, "I'm a roaring ripsnorter from a hurrah camp, and I can't be stepped on. I'm an angel from Paradise Valley an' a bad one, an' when I flop my wings here's a tornado loose. I'm a tough customer to clean up after. Give me some of your meanest whiskey, a whole lot of it, that tastes like bumblebee's stings pickled in vitriol. I swallowed a cyclone for breakfast, a powder mill for lunch and I haven't begun to

8)   To gamble.

to cough yet. Don't crowd me." And some years ago there was a neatly lettered sign over the bar in one of these many establishments. It read, "Let's have a drink to the man upstairs. He is the one who gives us the strength to enjoy our weaknesses." And, another, which strikes the memory: "Why do the Irish leave the country, why do they emigrate, they are all following the whiskey that's exported crate by crate."

Much of the business of some towns is still carried on in these bars. This is due partly to the basic fact that many of the town's leaders are the bartenders or bar owners. Even today many of the various mens clubs hold their regular meetings in these rendezvous. [9] Life for the local citizens, whether drinkers or not, is one perpetual imbibing experience and as a result everyone knows everyone's business, problems, aspirations and disappointments. It is, therefore, impossible for a visiting passerby not to overhear both private and municipal matters being discussed in these saloon-museums.

Modern day thirst parlor - The French in Gardnerville. Photo: Bret Duster.

9)   I remember vividly a number of Planning Commission meetings in Winnemucca that adjourned to one or another of the local bars for liquid sustenance while various matters were discussed and decisions reached. The chairman, an exemplary merchant of the town and the District Attorney usually led these (late night) determinations to highly successful conclusions. The current open meeting laws now forbid this.

TWO

THE NORTHERN

One of the truly great watering places in early day Nevada was the <u>Northern</u> <u>Saloon</u> in the small mining camp of Vernon. This gold camp was established in 1905 on a broad, gently sloping fan of the foothills of the Seven Troughs Range in the Seven Troughs Mining District in northern Pershing County, some 65 miles north of Lovelock. This District also included the towns of Mazuma, Seven Troughs, Farrell, and later, Tunnel. By 1910, all of the towns were dead (or almost) although some evidenced continued activity until as late as 1918. Today only a couple of buildings and inhabitants still remain at the New Tunnel, a few miles to the south ; all the other communities have eroded back into the sagebrush.

A "Northern" saloon existed in many early day Nevada places; it was a popular name for some reason. Perhaps the two best known was the original "<u>Goldfield</u> <u>Northern</u>" and the "<u>Northern</u>" in Rawhide, both emporiums instigated and owned by the famous promoter Tex Rickard. The <u>Goldfield</u> <u>Northern</u>, located at the intersection of Main and Crook Street was joined by the <u>Place</u> <u>Mohawk,</u> and <u>Heritage</u> (saloons) on the other corners. Lovelock, Ely, Ellendale and Beatty also had "<u>Northern</u>" saloons. Other common and popular saloon names, found in many camps, were <u>Delta,</u> <u>Tuscarora,</u> <u>The</u> <u>Pioneer</u> and <u>The</u> <u>Mint</u>.

The <u>Northern</u> <u>Saloon</u> was by far the best and most popular building in the district. It was also the largest. It was the coolest place during the summer and the warmest in the winter. It was a rather typical wooden structure of the day with the usual false front and a bank of windows on either side of an inset and sheltered doorway, but most importantly, it was the "club" and gathering place for everyone who could get there and everyone in the whole region managed to do so on a regular basis.

The owner, Ray Holbrook, and his Irish bartender provided an exceptional brand of friendliness and good will, whether you were a cash customer or merely a "looker". This was an important aspect, for the owner's personality and technique strongly typified the establishment. An operator undoubtedly had to be inherently tough, but most camouflaged this somewhat by an exterior air of conviviality and affability. They knew everyone in camp, they knew everything that was happening or going to happen, and they often mixed social duties in odd ways, including the conversion of the establishment on Sunday mornings for church services, after which the blanket covering the bar and the canvas covering the ubiquitous nude painting were quickly removed and the operation was again set up for further action.

Vernon was a typical "town" of the period. A great deal of mining activity spanned the state during the period following the 1905 and 1906 strikes, when such diverse bonanzas as Goldfield, Rhyolite, Fairview, Tonopah and Rawhide came into being. It was a volatile period, full of promise, and new towns were "springing up overnight" all over the state. Lots in Vernon originally sold for $75 hard cash. A post office soon opened and since the site was exceptionally arid, water was carted from nearby Seven Troughs for the princely sum of $6 (small keg), until the Vernon Water, Light and Power Company began operations in 1907.

<u>The Norther Saloon</u> in Vernon about 1907, with the Lovelock Stage waiting in front.
Photo: Nevada Historical Society.

The new water system, especially, was greeted with great joy since it was reported that there were usually a lot of dried bugs in the imported water which had to be screened out through one's teeth, although, as one miner said, "They were small and brittle and not at all offensive."

For over a year, Vernon served as the main commercial center of the entire Seven Trough District. It boasted 300 residents, a miner's union, a weekly newspaper [1], a hotel, one tent restaurant, a bank[2], a doctor and assay offices, even a stock exchange and a barber; although, it wasn't a real shop, only a chair inside the post office. "Fraction Bill," the barber, was also uncertain as to hours, usually being north in the hills searching for "fractions" of land left-over from claim locations. Haircuts were $1: a shave "four bits."

An eyewitness[3] of the period once reminisced that there was one time when Bill's absence was extremely vexing to his would-be customers. This occurred one Christmas Eve when a horde of hairy prospectors, fresh from their remote locations throughout the District, came to Vernon for some plentiful cups of Christmas Joy. First they flooded to the <u>Northern</u> (of course), to "cut the dust" and meet their old friends, but next they flocked next door to the barber in order to remove some truly outstanding growths of hair and whiskers. "Where the hell is Bill?" they demanded, not knowing that Bill had gone to Reno for his own celebration. Finally they turned to a wide-eyed young lad standing in the corner watching this growing dilemma, "How about you, son,

1) Supposedly a weekly—the editor spent so much time in the <u>Northern</u>, one could never really be sure it finally folded.
2) A small wooden structure operated by a gentle but dour Scotsman; a retired minister who sometimes tried to conduct church services in the building.
3) G. W. "Gus" Keller. *Reno Gazette*, February, 1958.

think you can cut my hair and shave me?" The boy didn't think so, but after some persuasion agreed, but only on the conditions of customer total acceptance, good or bad, and full payment regardless.

That started a long procession which lasted far into the night "The slaughter was terrible." After a few errant beginnings, that lad soon gained confidence and improved on the haircut part quite rapidly, but shaving those wiry beards was virtually impossible. Hardly a man wasn't cut. Most were cut often, and the supply of court plaster diminished rapidly. But there wasn't a single complaint; everyone took it as a huge joke and there was a great deal of ribald commentary and laughter at each bloody result. As each operation was concluded, the survivor paid gratefully (although sometimes ruefully) and immediately returned next door to the Northern, where they grouped themselves, with much laughter and raucous comment, into clubs of "one plaster," "two plaster," and even "three plaster" members, according to the markings on their faces. There was even one group of six veteran miners who sat off in one corner quite proud and aloof by themselves because only they could quality for the "five plaster" club.

Since the Northern was the cynosure of the region, it could be expected that important events, minor altercations and great conversations would emanate within its walls. Of the three, great conversations were the most normal and most interesting feature of the house. These ranged from the most elegant to the more hilarious. One night, for instance, two miners were discussing a remote strike one of them had made in extremely difficult terrain. The finder was greatly enthused about its prospects of great wealth. The other retorted, "I have made an examination of that mine and can say that the ore is there, that it assays high, and that it is there, in plenty, but to get your supplies in and your ore out, you will need a pack train of "Bauld Aigles."

The Northern was also the scene of most of the "goings on." One winter day a group were clustered about the big pot belly when one miner, who had during the afternoon consumed too much "redeye," drew his gun and waving it wildly, threatened to "shoot up the place." The Sheriff in short order appeared, disarmed the man and tossed his gun aside. The Sheriff then clamped the drunk's arms behind his and escorted him through the doors and out in the street. Then the real problem began for there wasn't a jail in Vernon. He called back into the saloon for a "bit of rope," and then tied the man to a handy pole saying, "There, maybe that will cool you off." Since the show seemed over, the rest of the patrons, who had observed the entire scene with avid interest, trooped back into the bar for more nourishment and warmth around the large, warm stove. It was a cold day with a stiff wind blowing from the flats. After about two hours, when it was almost dark outside, the Sheriff decided that his prisoner "probably had enough," but found the miscreant so cold and stiff that he had to carry him inside the building. He was set near the stove, fed some additional "redeye" and soon thawed out, apparently none the worse for wear at all and about in the same condition as when he started.

One of the most notable occurrences happened on the blustery wintry day when the door suddenly opened and shabby figure blew in with a gust of fine snow and a draft of chilling wind. He was new to the area; a ragged, dusty and bleary eyed bum with a face blue from the cold and clearly showing the many marks of a totally dissolute life. The man drew close to the stove, warming his hands, and a gentle steam began to emanate from his sorry looking clothes. Suddenly he turned to the assemblage, "Friends, he said, "I need a drink, but I am going to try to earn it. I shall recite a poem for you." Without waiting for a response, he then began a long recitation on the mother and lost son theme. The poem was cheaply sentimental, yet captivating, and everyone soon became quite engrossed. He spoke with great artistry in a deep and resonant voice with appropriate gestures and excellent timing. He finally finished to a totally silent audience. "Hell's fire," he said after a moment, "Who is buying me that drink?" This broke the ice; the remainder of the night was spent crowded close to the bar. The next day he disappeared.

The orator was W. Herman Knickerbocker, born in Louisiana, a former Methodist minister in New Orleans, who was tried for heresy, but acquitted. He then left religion, drifting to Tonopah where he built the Opera House, then to Goldfield, and later to Seven Troughs. He was well known in the Western Nevada as a promoter and orator, having gained considerable notice with an eloquent eulogy at the grave of one of Goldfield's most notorious female personages, as well as several other less noticed services, but it was really a year or so later that he went into the history books forever with his now famous epic oration for Riley Grannan, a gambler and plunger of Rawhide whom he barely knew.[4]

On April 3rd, the ex-preacher stood over the coffin in the tawdry back of a barroom, clad in the rough garb of a miner, facing the flotsam and jetsam of the desert, and brought tears to the eyes of this hardened crowd of men and women with his somewhat embittered comments on life, but delivered in a most flowery and oratorical manner. The address was full of references from Shakespeare complete with ringing phrases. It was dynamic; it was magnificent. He called Grannan (among other things) a "dead game sport" and a "public" benefactor who "smoothed the wrinkles from this brow of care and changed the moan into a song, wiped away the tears and replaced them with a jewel of joy." When he reached the climax he said, "And now I will say good-bye, Old Man. We will try to exemplify the spirit manifested in your life in bearing the grief of our parting. Words fail me here. Let these flowers, Riley, with their petaled lips and perfumed breath speak in beauty and fragrance the sentiments that are too tender for words...good-bye!"

Vernon also had a red-light district, a lone shack with a single occupant, off in the sagebrush and sufficiently remote to prevent any moral contamination. The social order then, as now, was relatively rigid. There was little apparent interaction between the town and the "friendly madam"—yet on certain festive occasions she would be allowed to become part of the community, if only for a day.

But by 1910, the boom was over! Vernon reached its peak in 1907-08 when it boasted a population of 600. By 1913, only about 50 persons resided in camp. The post office continued until 1918 mostly due to a continuing but small demand for ore during World War I. During the early 1920's, most of the buildings were moved to Tunnel, a newer camp two miles northwest of Vernon, however this operation, too, lasted but a short while.

The Northern disappeared—only a memory to the early wondrous days and the great people who made it so.

---

4) Riley Grannan was a bookmaker, known all over America; sometimes called the "Napoleon of the Betting Ring." His death was front page news.

A typical saloon scene. This one is in Tonopah about 1910. Everyone seems to be drinking beer.
Photo: Nevada Historical Society.

An early saloon in Searchlight, Clark County 1910. Photo: Carlos Morales.

Another very typical saloon interior. This is the J/K Saloon in Cherry Creek (in eastern Nevada) about 1905.[5]
Photo: Nevada historical society.

※ ※

"the water was certainly the worst ever had by man. Filtered through the comstock lead, it carried much of the plumbargo, arsenic cooperas and other poisonous minerals alloyed in that vein. The citizens of Virginia have discovered what they conceived to be an infallible way of correcting it; that is to say, was their practice to mix a spoonful of water in a half a tumbler of whiskey and then drink it. Even then the whiskey contained strychnine, oil of tobacco, tarantula juice and various poisons of the more general nature, including a dash of corrosive sublimate.

---

5)   The other saloon in Cherry Creek was The Exchange, owned by Dolph Sunberg..

THREE

THE BOX TENT SALOON

Saloons in Nevada desert towns often became doubly important because usually there was nothing to drink that wasn't in bottles. Nevada is the most arid state, averaging only about 7" of total precipitation a year, hardly enough to support the coyotes and jack rabbits, let alone hardrock prospectors. And in the more southerly areas of the state, the terrain and climate tend to become drier still.

One of the most arid sections of the state is that range of hills lying easterly of Walker Lake and extending into Ione Valley. This is the locale of such places as Dead Horse Wells, Rawhide, Gabbs Flat and other desolate points whose very names reflect the dry conditions. In 1907, at the height of the fever which hit the nation and state at the time, and spawned a gaggle of new diggings in this general area, a group of prospectors from Rawhide made a strike about 14 miles from that town which eventually became the famous Gold Pen, in operation for more than 20 years. By early 1908, a small "rush" to this district was underway. A new town called Bovard was laid out and it too was soon thriving with new miners and activity. Soon another group from Luning, Mina, and Hawthorne, surveyed another new townsite only about one mile from Bovard, which was duly christened Lorena.[1]

But Lorena did not have water. For that matter, neither did Bovard or Gold Pen, but those two older locations had engaged the services of a number of teamsters who where hauling water for those places. This service, by contract, soon also included Lorena, but the supply was irregular, often hap-hazard and sometimes non-existent. Towns were both flourishing and the many newcomers with dreams of untold wealth were buying property, erecting tents with abandon and drinking whiskey.

The main commercial enterprise in Lorena was, of course, the (Whiskey) Palace Saloon, which in this case was a "box-tent," a very common structure in these rural early towns. This edifice entailed wood sides at 3' high topped with a tent stretched tightly over frames. The floor remained packed dirt. Actually, it was a quite effective structure, resistant to the heavy winds and warm enough when the pot belly stove was fired up. The bar itself, as was also usual in such a new community, was only a plank laid across two barrels. Since the water situation was so uncertain, this bar thrived from its inception.

Soon a disproportionate amount of the newer activity seemed to trend towards Lorena, mostly due to the continuous and enthusiastic efforts of the local land agent who was anxious to sell as much property as possible. He even managed to induce a number of Bovard citizens to move— to Lorena. The future of this town indeed looked promising and there was great optimism, especially at the tent saloon. These actions did not escape the notice of the promoters and backers of Bovard.

---

1) Probably after that most popular Civil War song by that name.

Not a "box tent saloon" but close. This purely tent saloon flourished in Bovard, about one mile from Lorena in 1908. Photo: Courtesy of Nevada Historical Society.

So, one day the Lorena water wagons did not arrive. The town agent was acutely worried. He checked the liquid supply of every person in camp. There was practically none and there was no team available to get their own supply. What he did not know was that the Bovard promoters had bribed the teamsters not to carry water to their rival. After several more waterless days the situation was desperate, and reluctantly the decision was made to close down the town and move to Bovard. That evening all the citizenry of Lorena pooled their scanty resources for a "last supper." A somewhat stale ham bone was boiled in oatmeal with the last drops of water available, which made supper for everyone.

That night everyone packed to leave and at daybreak the men gathered sadly at the Whiskey Palace Saloon for their last breakfast. Flour and oatmeal were mixed into a batter, thinned with the last of the saloon beer supply and made into pancakes which almost all enjoyed, except the camp teetotaler, who mixed his with ginger-ale. There was no coffee, no juice, just dry pancakes in this dry arena.

An hour later the tents were down and the last die hard settlers of Lorena, with all their belongings packed on their backs, were strung out across the alkali flat toward Bovard, their hated rival. The saloon also moved; box, pole and barrels, where it prospered for a few months until Bovard, too, collapsed. Then everyone left and this site, too, reverted to sage, grease wood and a few tin cans. It is impossible to locate either one of them today.

Often the total community was comprised of tents. Building materials were difficult and expensive to come by—lumber cost $50/1,000 bd. ft. in California, but increased to $400-500/ 1,000 bd. ft. in Nevada. Most towns came and went rather swiftly; tents were highly mobile, and considerably cheaper than buildings. The picture below is a typical box tent facility—at Hornsilver a small mining camp, also in Esmeralda County, in 1908. (Photo: by Nevada Historical Society)

One of the best surviving pictures of a full scale box tent establishment is shown above. This business conglomerate operated in Gold Reef, a satellite digging in Nye County about six miles from Tonopah in 1907. The camp didn't last a year. Photo: Nevada Historical Society.

These tent saloons were not limited to the later southern areas of the Tonopah-Goldfield strikes. The picture below illustrates a similar structure in the northern reserves of Elko County.

Jack Hole-in Elko County, between Three Creek and Jarbidge at the confluence of Jack & Jenny Creeks on the road from Hollister, Idaho to Jarbidge, Nevada. Photo: The Northeastern Nevada Museum.

A tent restaurant in Esmeralda County 1906. Note the men dressed in white shirts, suits, and even vests. No mean feat in view of the environment. Photo: Nevada Historical Society.

FOUR

BIG SWEDE'S WHISKEY

The early issues of the *Record-Courier* (early Douglas County newspaper) are a bonanza of information, anecdotes and humorous incidents redolent of life of earlier times in Carson Valley. Surprisingly, the basis of these stories often parallels closely the current events and concerns of our time, but the style of reporting and the language are frequently much more "colorful" than at present. The following story in its entirety is from the February 18, 1908 issue of the *Record-Courier*:

The "Big Swede's" Whiskey "That's All"

During the past week or two the town has been overrun with drummers, mostly representatives of San Francisco and Sacramento concerns and a sprinkling of Eastern tenderfoot knights of the grip. One morning last week when business was a trifle quiet at the Gardnerville saloon and the "Big Swede" out of humor and a grouch for fair, one of the latter gentry came in and in plaintive tones inquired, "Pardon, but is this a Saloon?" Now if there's anything the Swede dislikes it is a dudish chap who is everlastingly using "Pardon me" and when asked the fool question if that was a saloon, the limit was reached. Gathering himself together, he handed the stranger a line of conversation something like this: "Is this a saloon? Why, you ham faced idiot, what do you think it is, a blacksmith ship? You must be the vice president of some ladies' sewing circle. Sure, it's a saloon—a barroom—a booze joint—a red-eye rendezvous. We've got the real stuff and if you want anything, step up and holler."

"What kind of whiskey have you got," he inquired?

"What kind of whiskey," echoed the Swede, "Why you rosy checked lummox, we've got all kinds of whiskey; we've got common ordinary everyday whiskey, the kind that killed father at the tender age of 95. We've got wisdom whiskey, the kind that makes the absorber think he's got Solomon backed off the map. Throw some of it under your belt and in ten minutes you'll be wondering why they didn't make you president instead of Teddy. We've got whiskerbroom whiskey, the kind that makes you throw a fit on the floor and when you get up you dust your clothes off with a whiskerbroom."

"We've got honest whiskey, the kind that causes a man to pay debts when he's drunk, and to kick him all over the lot when he's sober. We've got fool whiskey, the kind that causes your dear neighbor to lead you off somewhere in the Pine Nut Hills and whisper into your waiting ear a piece of news that was all over town the day before. Then we've got lovin' whiskey, the kind that makes some lobster waltz up to you, put his arm around your neck and blow a breath into your face that would drive a turkey buzzard away from a dead coyote or stampede the employees of a glue factory. We've got fighting whiskey, the kind that gets action on Tobe Ward or makes an Antelope Valley cowboy haul out his sixshooter and plug out the lights. We've got cryin' whiskey, the kind that makes a tenderfoot shed tears of anguish and sorrow whenever he hears a funny story. We've got sporting whiskey, the kind that makes you want to tackle the wheel or craps. Why, gol durn it, we've got the biggest stock in Nevada. If what I've mentioned ain't enough, why we'll give you some whoopin' whiskey, the kind that will make an undertaker jump his job and join a circus. We've got screamin' whiskey, the kind that makes a deaf mute scream for a job. We've got social whiskey, the kind that'll make a man who has given you the glassy eye for the past ten years hunt you up and give you the glad mitt; we've got family whiskey, the kind that makes a man go home and smash the furniture and call his mother-in-law unpleasant names. We've got"—but the tenderfoot was getting weak in the knees and faltered, "I'm a drummer for a whiskey house in Cincinnati, but guess you're stocked up. Good day." And the Swede says he wasn't halfway through the list yet.

"Big Swede" - actually Chris Jespersen, was born in Haal, Denmark in 1865 and come to America at an early age. He appeared (somehow) in Gardnerville at its very beginning and was resident when Gilman opened the first business house. During the ensuing years he worked as a carpenter, a teamster and a "whatever was available." He then entered the saloon business, served over the bar in many Gardnerville locations, most notable Papa Starkes, the Corner Bar and the J/T. In the process he became widely known throughout the State, altho most never knew his real name; he was simply "Big Swede". Later he served as a contract mail carrier and as the constable. A large, raw-boned man, he stood over 6 feet in height and weighed about 250 pounds and had a propensity for belligerency. He died in Gardnerville on 24 January, 1941, at 76 years, and is buried there.

"Big Swede's Bar" was in 1906 located on the corner of Main and Eddy Streets in Gardnerville, where the J/T Bar and Restaurant now operates. He also tended bar at The Corner (now Sharkey's) and The Oberon, which is now defunct. Note the arcaded porch - a distinct asset which has now been removed.
Photo: Carson Valley Historical Society.

"Big Swede" bar today! The interior of the J/T Saloon in Gardnerville, 1991. "Little" Jean, the owner and bartender (with the beret and glasses) is quite a contrast. Photo: Bret Duster.

⊰ ⊱

On a back page of a 1916 newspaper appeared the following recipe for a popular potion "guaranteed to make a jackrabbit spit in a bull dog's ear" (results not always guaranteed).

How to make "Ripgizzard":
    Mix -
            One peck meal
            Ten pounds sugar
            Two-three pounds dried apples
            Five gallons of water (ditch)

Set same on back of stove, or in the sun to ferment two to three days. Drink.

THEN…a Tuscarora saloon interior in September 1907. A Mr. Detheridge is the bartender.
Photo: Nevada Historical Society.

AND NOW…Centerville Bar – Carson Valley. Photo: Bret Duster.

FIVE DEFUNCT SALOONS IN DOUGLAS

Gardnerville and Minden, two small adjacent towns, in the green Carson Valley of Douglas County were hardly the expected location for some especially interesting early day "watering places." But there were five such saloons—all now defunct—which once provided an extra measure of sociability and character in this farming community. The oldest of these was the "Pony (Express) Saloon."

There are no "old timers" still left who remember the Pony Saloon. The only clear written reference relates: "1861-62, the Pony Saloon (Station), a first class house eight miles south of Carson City. Chet Benedict proprietor. Sharp Beer, also fine wines, liquors and cigars. This was a station on the Pony Express Route." (Van Sickle collection, in the Douglas County Library). That doesn't really tell much. It certainly doesn't indicate exactly where it was located and there is some uncertainty as to its precise location. It is speculated, however, that it was north of the Carson River somewhere along the base of Indian Hills, where the Pioneer Trail veered easterly on the route between Genoa and Carson City. There are a number of springs in this area, any one of which would appear a likely location. One source places it about one-fourth mile northerly of the Cradlebaugh Bridge Crossing on the Desert Road. (A) There are several old poplars and some willows at this point, usually indicating some previous human habitation. This, however, would be southerly of the Desert Road intersection with the Pioneer Trail, rather unlikely under the circumstances. Another locates it on the easterly slopes of Indian Hills, slightly south of Stewart (approximately opposite the Minimum Security Prison, (C), while still another locates it near the present day Sorensen Kennels, (B) This is the most likely spot since it would then be able to service the traffic on both the Desert Road and the Emigrant Trail to Genoa.

The sketch map indicates these various possible locations.

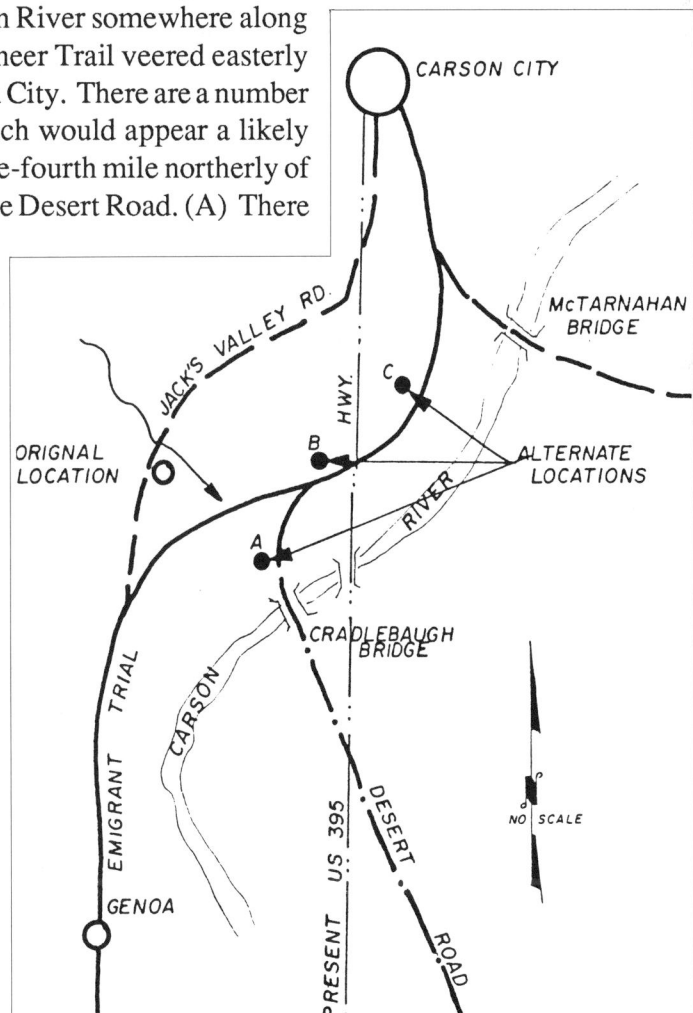

At any rate, wherever it was, it did not originate there. The original bar, according to an interview with an early day rancher, was in Jacks Valley "after you crossed the crick, where it (the road) started to climb the hills, some trees were right where it was located." This establishment, prior to 1861, was owned by Fulstone and operated by a Mert Seamon, although some others, probably bartenders, named Allison Rossiter and "Little Pete" were also in evidence. It was then called, appropriately, Jacks Valley Saloon. As traffic patterns changed, especially after the construction of Cradlebaugh Bridge in 1861, the entire building was moved—literally dragged down into the valley-to operate under the new name of the <u>Pony Saloon</u> and under the aegis of "Tony Bowers."

Thomas (Tony) Bowers was a colorful character of the day. Born in Ireland in 1832, he came to America when he was 17, drifting to Nevada in the early 1860's. He was closely associated with the Fulstone Ranch properties in Jacks Valley for many years and also established a "station" on the Glenbrook Grade known as "Saint's Rest." He is listed in the voters' record of 1882 and in 1890 owning property with an assessed valuation of $100. Tony Bowers was also an uncle of Jim Kane, the famous stage coach driver (in whose home he died on 8 January 1911). Bowers operated the Pony for many years from its inception in 1861 (or 1862), until about the turn of the century. By 1902, a new person, a Mr. William Seaton, was in charge.

The building was most unpretentious, just a single one story wood weather-beaten structure, about 25' x 40', beside the trail. It had the usual hitching post and a watering trough—little else. It did serve drinks, food and offered a welcome respite, for a few moments, from the dusty and long drive to Carson for supplies, medical treatment, services—or whatever.

By a lucky chance an old photograph was recently found that purports to be the remnants of this building. Dated in the 1930's, it shows little but two Mormon poplar trees flanking a heap of lumber. By matching the horizon and mountain profile, it appears that the location was in Jacks Valley, but the site could not be found, and the location does not match several eyewitness remembrances of local old timers, all of whom indicate alternate "B" as the definite location. There are, of course, no remains, however the existence of ample spring water here would tend to verify this site.

There is no record of its closure, however a 1916 newspaper mentioned its continuing existence, so it must have been later than that. By 1910 the V & T Railroad had detoured most of the freight traffic and earlier valley wagon roads were rapidly falling into disuse.

There were no reported disorders there, no flagrant murders, or other events apparently worth noting by the local papers. It was just a roadside rest stop and now only a forgotten thread in the tapestry of time. One of the few written references appeared in an early issue of the Genoa Courier, which stated:

Thunder and Lighting

A. H. Davis has just returned from Jacks Valley, and says that another terrific thunderstorm has passed through that section. A thunderbolt struck 60 feet from him, throwing him out of his buggy, knocking him senseless. The horse was paralyzed for twenty minutes. Rocks were unpheaved and the sand was thrown 100 feet in the air. Trees were torn up and the ground was rent 100 feet deep. Two piute Indians and two cows are reported to have been killed further up the valley. The thunder cloud was about an acre in area.–*Carson Appeal.*

A special to the Courier from Jacks Valley states that the origin of the thunderbolt has been traced to a bottle which came from the Pony Saloon.

There were a reported ten saloons in Gardnerville between 1900 and 1920, where ample doses of tangle foot would be taken aboard and where one could "bait the tiger" with impunity. For a rural, one dirt street town that did not exceed 200 people, all of whom were very conservative farmers of strong German and Danish descent, this was most unusual. Most of these places were devoted to serious beer drinkers, especially the many hands who were working on the surrounding ranches during the summer months. It was not unusual for each ranch to have as many as 50 extra hands during this period. These were the days before machinery made it a much simpler affair. One of the most interesting of these many saloons was that "Palace of Pleasure"–The Oberon, later called Germania. It was located on the north side of Main Street in Gardnerville, about opposite the three story Ritchford Hotel. Since the Ritchford was the leading hostelry, as well as the Carson Valley Station for the stages southerly to the Aurora and Bodie Mines, the siting was quite conducive to a constant and lucrative trade.

The Oberon was originally operated by Rice and Neddenriep; later it was sold to Jarvis and Barnett in 1903, and then operated by Barnett alone. During those years, it was a very active and popular spot, as the many ads in the *Record-Courier* at the time support. In early 1904, its operation was assumed by Messrs. Jim Beck and Al Daudel, whose proprietorship was also prosperous, and continued until about 1910. No doubt, the business was aided considerably by their intriguing and somewhat tongue in cheek ads, several of which follow:

The Oberon...

ALL outward application of the infallable awaken curiosity. Curiosity stirs the sluggish brain to action, the active brain arouses the torpid system and health reanimates the sluking frame. For further particulars visit the OBERON and partake of Cutter whiskey which is a cure for all ills the human flesh is heir to. Our Competitors are gentlemen whom we honor and respect. We don't expect all the business; what we ask is, DROP IN, sit down and read the papers and say hello. We are your friends whether you trade with us or not.

NIGGER POOL A SPECIALTY.

The Oberon

A Palace of Pleasure

At the time we obtained possession of the above resort, a rear view of our trousers did not resemble a fringe factory; on the contrary, we started right—got off on the right foot.—People are coming our way, we cater to the multitude. Extend the Jolly "Mitt" to every one. Even if the brightest smile does not come from a happy heart, the smiles we dispense over our bar are sufficient to drive the gloomy dope from anyone. Call in and partake there of—try our renowned cure.

SIGNED

Jim Beck   **Al Daudel**

Papa Starke behind his bar – <u>The Oberon</u> – in Gardnerville, circa 1906. Photo: Nevada Historical Society.

During this same period, one of the more popular counter men in the area was "Papa" Starke, who was active in various places around Gardnerville, and in Carson City. It is somewhat difficult to trace all of his movements since there was a brisk exchange of ownership, proprietorship, cooks and bartenders in those days. However, he apparently was at the Gardnerville Hotel for a while and then operated at the Corner Saloon, (now Sharkey's) which he called "Papa's Place," featuring a chop house with meals at all hours.

Starke sometimes advertised in German, as was the custom of the day. Typical is this ad which appeared in the September 9, 1904, issue of the *Record-Courier*:

> Papa's Place. The Corner Saloon. Solche Gaeste will ich haben die stets friendsam disen rien. Essen, Trinken, zahlen, gern und dan ruhig abmashiven, thness nuench ich fried und gluech kehren sie zu mir zuruch. September 9, 1904.

Papa Starke was born in Dortsfield, Germany, March 29, 1860, coming to Carson Valley in 1893. When he first arrived he had a little hand organ, his sole possession, with which he made his living. He then worked as a cook in several hotels and operated a bakery at Rahbecks' Gardnerville Hotel and in Carson City at various times. He was married and had a son, born in 1887, but who died in 1910, and a daughter. Papa Starke was a huge man, weighing well over 250 pounds and was quite husky. He was a baker by trade. His face was heavily pockmarked and he had a large nose, a thoroughly frightening aspect to the small fry of the town; however, he had a kindly disposition, loved all children inordinately, and was forever giving them cookies and other goodies from his ovens. Papa also had a particularly articulate parrot, a large green bird with an outstanding and very profane vocabulary which was of great entertainment to the patrons, but a constant source of embarrassment to all women. The parrot could swear equally well in both German and English and was often heard to even cuss Papa out. Papa spoke in a quite broken, coarse German accent, often mixing German and English indiscriminately; however, his wife spoke excellent English until she became excited or flustered when she, too, would engage in the same mixture.

In 1908, he transferred his activities to the Club Hotel, returning to the Corner Saloon in the spring of 1909. In October, 1909, Papa went to Germany, returning in the spring of 1910, with an immense music box, a true nickelodeon. It featured colored glass, a waterfall, various instruments and drums. Upon his return, Starke moved to the Oberon, changing its name a year later to the Germania. Papa installed his music box as a major feature of his new establishment, where it went night and day—very loudly—at 5 cents/play. The establishment soon became the social center of town and remained so for many years. It was during these years that Papa's Place became famous throughout the area to the point were Papa could and did advertise, "Our lunch counter is par excellence, of course our bar goes without mention, because...Papa Starke owns it!"

Starke was a great lover of "tricks" and usually had something going. He usually had all kinds of things on the bar. One was a jar of raspberry jam. If the lid was removed, a "snake" would pop out. Other contrivances exploded when opened or otherwise would cause consternation. One of the more bizarre aspects was the "Devil's Hole," a small basement space which was "dark as a dungeon" but was rigged to emit strange noises. This was a frightening but delicious attraction to the children. Sometimes he had a skeleton dangling from the floor joists.

This operation featured a 24 foot long bar with an extremely fancy back bar and a polished mirror, extending to the ceiling, which contrasted strongly with the fresh sawdust on the floor. An excellent "free" bar lunch was also standard. It was extensive, featuring crackers, cheese, bologna, salami and plenty of it. The main treat was wursts, any and all kinds, but especially liverwurst. Papa loved German sausages and wursts, always highly seasoned. There was also dancing, since women were welcome, and a few card tables (solo and cribbage), but no gaming.

The OBERON
HOTEL AND SALOON

First Class Lunch Counter

We Mean at all Times to Please

The Best is None Too Good

Try Our 25 Cent Meals

"PAPA" STARKE

Gardnerville, Nevada

During the early days of World War I, Papa Starke's Saloon was the headquarters of the pro-German elements in the valley, of which there were quite a few. The Bund met regularly, sometimes twice a week, in the back room. In March 1916, it was still called the Germania

(Starke, proprietor), however, in April 1916, Starke suddenly appeared as proprietor of the Centerville Saloon. It was short lived—only a month later—he was back at the Germania, taking over operation of Starke's Cafe and Bakery, featuring fresh pastry and cafe meals. Following its sale, Starke continued to live in a little house behind the bar. He became quite ill and destitute during his later years and died on the 6th of January, 1946.

And then there was the single saloon in the nearby town of Minden, a mile to the west. Minden was a totally different community; a preplanned "new town"—very unique for that 1906 date which was constructed as a total project by the Dangberg interest, a large ranching operation who owned the land.

When Minden was being formulated, a special concern was the proliferation of drinking establishments, especially in nearby Gardnerville, where there were multiple saloons offering "whiskey, wines and fine cigars" to the populace, both permanent and passing through. The Dangberg Company met this concern by establishing very tight controls through the use of restrictive covenants (deed restrictions) which stated:

> "that the parties hereto for themselves, their heirs, successors and legal representatives, hereby agree that intoxicating liquor shall never be manufactured, sold or otherwise disposed of as a beverage in any place of public resort in or upon the premises hereby granted or any part thereof."

These covenants were applied on an individual (lot) basis rather than the more common "blanket" coverage of today. These restrictions for the most part carry to this day; the sale of liquor is still severely restricted in Minden!

With the growth of Minden during the next few years and the "distance" to the bars in Gardnerville, this prohibition soon became increasingly onerous. "There simply had to be a place where people could go and meet and talk over things of common interest, " reported the local paper. "Since H. F. Dangberg launched the Minden townsite project, it has been generally believed the town would remain dry as far as saloons were concerned, but this week that assumption has been disproved by the announcement and commencement of a thirst parlor in that town. Fritz Dangberg will conduct the new resort and the building is already underway. [1] It is to be a two story frame building with the upper floor containing ten rooms for eight lodgers. The new venture will be rushed to completion in order to be ready for summer business (*Record-Courier*, May 7, 1909).

So on 14 May 1909, F. C. (Fritz) Dangberg, former (longtime) proprietor of the Valhalla Bar in Gardnerville, was permitted to open the Heidelberg (bar) on Esmeralda Street. This, it was reported, was because it was "almost necessary" and because Mr. Dangberg had exhibited a "well known ability to conduct a first class resort.

---

1)   It was generally recognized at the time that the Dangberg interests were not enthused about the exodus of their employees to the Gardnerville saloons and therefore decided to operate their own parlor-in Minden-even to the point of forbidding their employees (on threat of dismissal) to continue to go to Gardnerville.

This new "thirst parlor" originally was established on the southerly side of Esmeralda Street on the corner of 3rd Street. Business was good, and by means of thrift and hard work, Mr. Dangberg found it possible to erect the brick building in Minden that is now known as the Pony Express Restaurant and moved the operation across the street to this new location in 1910.

The new Heidelberg Saloon was fashioned after an old German tavern with keg beer and beer in quart bottles available at all times. The saloon was also conveniently located across the street from the Minden depot, (a terminus) of the Virginia & Truckee Railroad, and was not only a meeting place for his friends, but also a gathering place for visitors and business men coming to the valley on the railroad.

A 1912 map indicates the Heidelberg Saloon here as well as a barber shop and a card room. It was still operating as late as 1916. Later this building housed a small market and soda fountain (Triangle Lunch & Bar) operated for many years by John Ellis.

The second bar in Minden did not operate until five years later in 1917 when the Minden Inn was formally opened (on June 11th) just in time for that summer's Carson Valley Days Celebration. It, too, is closed now and the only old saloon still operating in Minden is the (new) Pony Express located where the old Heidelberg once was.

The Heidelberg about 1910. Photo: *Record-Courier*.

One of the earliest colorful saloons along the east slope was "Hansen Saloon" in Genoa, located on the main street in the middle of town. This hospitable hostelry was a local favorite. It opened about 1862, as the Metropolitan, but the name changed in 1886, when T. ("Tige") Hansen took over. Hansen was an ex-woodcutter and a native of Denmark; many of his patrons were his old cronies from his logging days, essentially a very rowdy bunch. Hansen purveyed "good wet goods" and often proclaimed that "the genial Tige will treat you right".

This building, along with most of the rest of town burned down in the great fire of 1910.

Interior of Tige's Saloon. Photo: Nevada Historical Society.

This apparently was an extremely satisfactory place and one which truly merited the title of "A real Old Nevada Saloon."

The <u>Corner Bar</u> in Gardnerville was a popular spot for the hay crews.
This is now the site of Sharkey's Casino and Restaurant.
Photo: Carson Valley Historical Society.

The fifth earlier important, but now replaced drinking spot, was the very popular <u>Corner Saloon</u> located at the corner of School and Main Streets in the Town of Gardnerville. This is now the site of <u>Sharkey's</u>, a local casino and restaurant. In the earlier days, in Carson Valley, before the use of machinery, the ranches all kept large haying crews during the summer. The work was dry and tedious, the weather then rather hot, and as a consequence some tremendous thirsts ensued which were frequently assuaged by the many saloons which then lined Main Street around the turn of the century.

ᚼ ᚽ

One young prospector complained one day that Nevada was "an unhealthy place to live"; his companion, an old grizzled veteran replied "and an unhealthy place to die, too."

SIX

ROBBERY AT THE BUTLER[1]

One would think that saloons due to their prominence, obvious cash flow and general lack of security, would be easy targets for robbers. Most early Nevada towns were seriously isolated, making getaways difficult, which intended to discourage this activity. Strangely, the record of saloon robbery is not great. They were in fact surprisingly few, probably reflecting the unique positions of esteem the local saloons held in the community.

But one such robbery occurred in the <u>Butler</u> (saloon) in Tonopah ,[2] then and now an active mining camp, one bitterly cold night just after midnight on January 19, 1903. The bar that evening had been rather quiet and there were only a few customers still remaining when two masked men with two cocked guns entered through the back door and ordered all present "to raise their hands, then place them palms down on the bar," as though having a drink. A wave of the guns reinforced the following admonition that "no one will be hurt if all remained in that position." One of the two then gave his pistol to his companion and then stepped behind the long bar were he found the door to the big safe securely locked, while the second man, with guns in hand, positioned himself behind the door. He then cleaned out the cash register (ringing up "no sale)." He noticed an unusual diamond ring on one of the faro dealers and promptly appropriated it and then dumped all the silver dollars from the gaming table into his sack. At this moment another incipient imbiber, a Bill Anderson, wandered in through the front door and was instantly ordered to assume the same position at the bar. George Cole, one of the owners (and bartender), decided to "flee the scene" before he might be forced to open the safe; he dashed for the door and quickly ran into the street. But, as he ran, the second robber posted at the door fired at him at point blank range. Cole was bent over nearly double and the bullet entered at the base of his scalp and furrowed through causing a painful but not really serious wound. Cole staggered, but continued running with the second robber now close behind. Cole, shouting for help, finally reached the town fire bell which he began to ring wildly.

Meanwhile, the first bandit, still in the bar, smiled and calmly remarked, "Now, boys, I'll show you how to take a faro bank without placing a bet." He then opened the drawer and $400 in gold went into his sack. He then smiled again, opened the door and fled into the darkness.

Within two minutes the premises were jammed with spectators, customers and police. A posse was quickly organized and the hunt was on throughout the rest of the night on the icy and steep streets of Tonopah. But to no avail, not a trace was ever found of the two cool bandits.

---

1) This saloon was named after Jim Butler, prominent miner, promoter and citizen who reportedly founded the town. But that is another story.

2) Most robbers found the stages much more attractive. In 1880, Marietta, not far from Tonopah, boasted 13 saloons, none of which were ever robbed. The daily stage was robbed 30 times that same year, the high point being four times in one week!

This unnamed saloon in Tonopah (it could easily have been the Butler) was an active place in 1901. Note the dapper bartender, the brass rail, the ubiquitous spittoons and the very ornate back bar – all typical of the times.
Photo: Nevada Historical Society.

A more recent drinking parlor exhibiting a much more relaxed state.
This was the bar in the Ore House Saloon in Ione, also in Nye County.
Unfortunately, it is now closed, but it is not forgotten. Photo: By the
author.

~ SEVEN ~

BULLDOG KATE AND HOG EYED MARY

Many of the women who first followed the gatherings of men in the early Nevada mining camps were equally as tough and disreputable as the men or perhaps even more so! They had to be in order to survive at all in that primitive environment. Usually they were fairly low down on the social and monetary scale as well. These women tended to be obstreperous, vile mouthed, antagonistic and usually heavily addicted to strong drink—usually gin—and when in the "cups," which was as regular as possible, they were most belligerent. This could and often did lead to altercations and disturbances. A prime example concerns the "disagreement" between one Kate Miller (otherwise known by the uncomplimentary sobriquet of "Bulldog Kate") and Mary Irwin (otherwise known as "Hogeyed Mary," an equally disparaging appellation), both denizens of the burgeoning camp of Eureka in east central Nevada, who came to a major confrontation on the night of August 3, 1876.[1]

Silver ore was first discovered in the area in September 1864. However, the town did not really begin to grow until 1870. The well known *Eureka Sentinel* began publication in that year, stage and freight lines became more frequent, and several large mining companies were established. Following the completion of the Eureka and Palisade Railroad in October 1875, the camp became an important transportation center for most of eastern Nevada, including such isolated satellite locations as Tybo, Austin, Belmont, Pioche and Hamilton.

By 1876 the town supported almost one hundred saloons, many gambling parlors, several theaters, a wide variety of churches, boarding houses and stores. It was a full grown city by Nevada's standards, especially for that day, and had all the expectations of continued and future greatness so common to that period.

"Bulldog Kate" (this cognomen was a fair index of her general behavior and reputation) was spending that Saturday evening at Cramer's Saloon, one of the profusion of such parlors on Main Street, drinking, watching a game of pedro[2] then in progress at a back table, and in general "carrying on" with the other patrons. She had, it is said, some years before been an "honest washerwoman" in Denver City, Colorado, with a husband and two children until some other woman, jealous of her for some reason, had poisoned both children, leaving her embittered and with an attitude that "the world was her enemy." She was much addicted to strong drink, had an especially vile tongue, and a bad reputation, being generally recognized as "dangerous and quarrelsome."

---

1) Such nicknames, especially for women of the demimonde were usual. In Reno about this same time were: Cockeyed Liz, Too two Jonny, Russian Sophia, Big Mouth Annie, French Lou, Tar Flat Jenny, Whiskey Mabel. Bunko Moll, Bible Backed Annie and the Carson Banger.

2) A Basque card game.

Little is known of Hogeyed Mary, except that she had plied her chosen trade[3] in Central Nevada for at least eight years and was generally known to be "peaceable, but occasionally prone to drink."

Apparently a strong ill feeling had existed between the two for some time. By 11:00 P.M. Kate was drunk and quite noisy and when Mary entered they began by waging a whiskey war of words. This finally led to Kate asking Mary "What she was going to do?" "I'm going to lick you, " responded Hogeyed Mary. Both rose and started for the door together, however, before they got there, Mary turned, seized Kate around the throat, whipped out a knife from the folds of her dress, and repeatedly slashed into the body of Kate, effecting several severe wounds, the worst of which was in the abdomen where her bowels protruded. Kate collapsed and was taken back into the room, surrounded now by a large crowd which magically appeared (as usual). A doctor was called, but Kate died the following Sunday at 3:00 A.M.

Hogeyed Mary was immediately incarcerated in the Eureka Jail where she languished several months, pending the trial scheduled for the 14th of December, 1876. She was charged with murder in the first degree. "Both women of the town and both notoriously dissolute characters. Both had been repeatedly in the police files and had several times been in the County Jail for boisterous conduct," reported the local paper, accurately but succinctly .

The surviving written local newspaper accounts of the proceedings are somewhat sketchy. In frustration (and desperation). The County Clerk in Eureka County was concerned on the off-hand chance that there might still be a buried file on the trial . There was indeed, and Ms. Marcia Elliot, Deputy Clerk, was so kind as to find, deep in the records of the County, the original handwritten transcript of the proceedings, and to transcribe it in its entirety, together with some notes. It seems that the trial was duly held on December 14, 1876, in Eureka, with Judge Cole presiding. The proceedings required the full day and a long parade of witnesses appeared, many of whom were either present in the saloon where it happened, or nearby, and eye witnesses to the action. These included Mr. A. C. Bishop, Deputy Sheriff Long, Constable McGee and a number of male patrons including the pedro players and two loungers who were sitting on the bench outside. Their testimony was followed by a similar parade of female witnesses, many with names like "Spanish Woman" and "Belle" Rogers, all of whom testified that Bulldog Kate was a terrible person who "had a reputation for being a fighter," and whose character was rough and dangerous. In direct contrast, the defendant, Mary Irwin, was described by eleven different witnesses as: "never being quarrelsome or in trouble, " "her reputation is good, " "she is a good woman" (but sometimes drinks), and " I knew her for seventeen years and never knew her to have any trouble." She has always been very quiet, her character is good, " etc. Cramer, the saloon owner, also testified that "after Kate was stabbed and lying on the table in my saloon, " she said: "I did not expect the damned woman would kill me, but I brought it on myself." This was corroborated by witness George A. Burres who stated that: "Kate then said, Hogeyed Mary, the bitch, has killed me, but I think I deserved it."

---

3) Which was, of course, prostitution.

After an absence of 18 hours in seclusion, the jury failed to agree and were thereupon discharged by the Judge. The local paper, quoted by the *Territorial Enterprise*, December 19, 1876, stated: "We understand that the jury stood nine for acquittal and three for conviction. The results of the jury's deliberations was a surprise as the general impression prevailed that a conviction would be secured.

The case is set for retrial at the February term of the court and bail of the prisoner was fixed at $10,000."

At that point all further local newspaper accounts of the matter stopped, although, a number of key issues of the paper are missing. A diligent perusal of the *Eureka Sentinel* for the first six months of 1877 failed to reveal any mention of the case or its disposition. Nor was there any mention in the *Territorial Enterprise*.

The second trail was held on the 5th of February, 1877. The simple verdict was handwritten on a scrap of paper torn from a larger sheet. The verdict, (quoted exactly from Eureka County records was):

> "Eureka, Nevada
> February 5th, 1877
> We, the Jury, find the Defendant
> not guilty.
>
> Thomas J. Read
> Foreman"

Since a large number of eye witnesses observed this act of murder, this verdict is hard to accept unless one also accepts the frontier concept concerning the goodness (or badness) of the relative "characters" of Bulldog Kate and Hogeyed Mary, disagrees that Bulldog Kate was indeed a "real bad dude" and deserved to die, and the net gain was somehow worth it. It certainly is a very interesting, if naive, approach to the rule of law.

Apparently there were a number of other such dissolute female characters frequenting the streets and numerous bars of Eureka at that time. There was a Madam Laura Henrietta Lake, for instance. She was, or was reported to be, a lady of "distinguished connections" in San Francisco, but she was often prone to allow her vivacious (and voracious) appetite for gin to get the better of her judgement. She announced one night, for instance, in the most belligerent tone, that she was "Terror #1" for that portion of Nevada, and immediately reinforced that claim by her frantic efforts to carve and slaughter the entire neighborhood. She was finally collared and hauled before the local court where she was fined $60 or 30 days internment. She chose internment.

Then there was a Mrs. Leach who was also a well known local with highly developed belligerent propensities, especially under the influence of a drop of the "craythur." She, too, was in due time apprehended and fined $50 or 21 days in the County Jail. However, in consideration of promises of future good behavior, she was released on her own recognizance (one wonders how well these promises were kept).

It is not possible to overlook Mrs. Nixon who was also an obstreperous, vituperative female who, had, during her many drunken tirades on Main Street, afforded great amusement to those who were not the subject of her obscene abuse. It is reported that she "celebrated the 4th of July, 1877, with some gusto, imbibing a couple of glasses of beer which had such an effect on her nervous system that she was completely overcome." The rest of the town, who had less respect for the subtle amenities of the English language, called her "plain drunk." At any rate, she finally removed her clothing to a point that "Mother Eve in a fig leaf was fully dressed by comparison." This caused some embarrassment on the part of the Sheriff, but he finally managed to get her adorned sufficiently to take her off to the local poky where she was fined $75 or 37 days in the County Jail. Her total capital was (by then) only $2 but she offered grandly to "soak" a watch to the Judge who, however, was "obliged to decline the speculation."

Mining-even existing-in early day Nevada, was an extremely difficult endeavor. This scene, in Nye County about 1901, about a year after the discovery of Tonopah illustrates clearly the situation.
Photo: Nevada Historical Society.

EIGHT

THE SALOON THAT BECAME A CITY

In the very early days a saloon developed in the middle of Mason Valley, in Lyon County, with absolutely no particular reason for it being there. The operation was simply called "Willow Switch" because of the sturdy framework of willows that framed the structure. The tule roof and the dirt floor were all in keeping with the general harmony and spirit of the place. At any rate, it was a most popular gathering place for most of the male population of the area. For 10 cents a cup a cowboy could quickly forget his daily problems. But, because the liquid dispensed was so powerful, he literally took a great chance to even drink the stuff. Only the most intrepid drinker dared to have a second.

One Horton Aldrich was the owner and barkeep. He was a most ingenious manager who firmly believed in the "bottomless" cup. Accordingly, when the whiskey barrel became low, he compensated by doctoring the contents with anything available. Chewing tobacco, liniments, various flavorings, turpentine, even raw alcohol was added indiscriminately to the potion. The end result, as can well be imagined, was incredible and never exactly the same, yet no one complained, and he prospered.

In 1869, William Lee, originally from Kentucky, purchased 160 acres to the immediate south. Several years later a store was built on this land and soon thereafter another saloon was erected across from this (Bennet's) store. Since those were the only buildings, the complex informally became known as the "Switch." The newer saloon keeper, a Mr. James Downey, deciding to improve on Aldrich's offering, went to Virginia City and obtained a recipe for liquor which proved so potent that the imbibers (mostly tough cowboys) began to call the stuff "pizen." It was not long before Jim Downey's saloon gained all the business, the old Willow Switch Bar closed and activity centered on this new "Switch."

One day a fancy carriage with a full "fringe on top", and pulled by two fine horses, was stalled behind a huge herd of cattle being driven through the valley. A well dressed and well bred Englishman stepped out and asked the nearest cowboy where he might find a Mr. James Downey who lived, as he understood, in a place called "Pizen Switch." The cowboy thought the name most appropriate and rapidly spread it among his cohorts. The name soon caught on with the populace, and soon the press and residents alike were calling it just "Pizen Switch." A crudely painted sign erected at the crossroads soon attested to that fact. There was, however, some continuing dissatisfaction with this colorful name, especially with the growing feminine portion of the community. This eventually led to the re-naming of the town to "Greenfield," in November, 1872, complete with a committee specifically organized to "scalp" anyone who referred to its earlier appellation.

About this same time, the Carson and Colorado Railroad was making plans to extend a narrow gauge line from Mound House[1] to Walker Lake. This was completed in 1881 with Wabuska, at the north end of Mason Valley, as an established station on the line.

When a rumor circulated through the valley that this was to become a full scale standard gauge track, a petition was prepared to change the name of the town (again), this time to "Yerington" in the hope that Hume Yerington, the Superintendent of the railroad, would extend the track into the town. The name was duly changed, but the scheme failed. Mr. Yerington gravely accepted the honor and presented the community with a large American Flag, but the railroad stayed where it was.

The original name a tribute to insobriety as well as a colorful image directly from the old west, still lurks in the dusty background and is, even yet, occasionally heard today in such local business names as the "Pizen Switch Laundry and Carwash," and "Pizen Switch Motors."

⧨ ⧩

When the Western Pacific Railroad built its line through Elko County in 1908, they identified a shipping point for livestock from Clover and Ruby Valleys at a place about 20 miles south of Wells in eastern Nevada. A saloon soon opened to serve the construction workers and the area cowboys. The bartender painted a simple sign one day reading "to bar" pointing it in the direction of the establishment. The railroad officials, searching for a name for their new town, then called it Tobar. The town peaked in 1916 with two saloons, a rooming house, hotel, hardware store, lumberyard, blacksmith, two stores, school, post office and newspaper. The name was changed to Clover City in 1918 – but there is nothing left today.

---

1) Which was the connection to the V & T Railroad Line to Virginia City.

NINE

THE OLDEST SALOON IN NEVADA

Genoa, in Douglas County, has the distinction of being the "oldest" community in the State and therefore has the oldest saloon, since that was usually the first activity in town. This hamlet, tucked against the escarpment of the Carson Range of the Sierra Nevada, is still a vibrant and viable town with a certain often disputatious character. The oldest still active bar is the Genoa Bar and it certainly looks the part. Situated in "downtown" Genoa (one of perhaps three or four remaining commercial buildings), this throwback to the territorial days features high embossed tin ceilings, tall narrow doors and an old bar and back bar adorned with the usual collection of trivia and junk. It is a popular tourist attraction and plump ladies in tight shorts, plump men with colored hats and assorted others, all with cameras around their necks[1], are prevalent at all hours. The bartender can sometimes be cantankerous, which is part of its mystique and fits the total picture, somehow.

Interior: Genoa Saloon, 1991.
Photo: Bret Duster.

Bob Carver – The sometimes irascible owner and barkeep.
Photo: Bret Duster.

1) Taking pictures of the interior is no longer permitted.

<u>Genoa Bar</u>. Taken in the late 1940's – but still exactly the same. Photo: By Jim Lawrence.

TEN

EARLY SALOON "CHIEFS"

At the beginning of the Nevada experience, from 1860 to 1866, the Nevada Territory spawned a particular type of villain found nowhere else, the so- called "saloon chief." There was very little organized law during that time. The only regulations were whatever the more responsible settlers developed and adhered to voluntarily. It was a time when everyone from lowliest mucker to diamond strewn nabob went fully armed on all occasions. Usually this was the famous "six shooter," however, some men elected to carry two of them and frequently also a big bowie knife.

Horse stealing and counterfeiting were considered the most heinous crimes. Footpads were classed as the lowest of criminals and their capture often resulted in a speedy hanging. Saloon chiefs—the saloon bully—were generally acknowledged as the "prime bad men," and they were quite proud of this designation. Each designated "chief" usually ruled a particular saloon which became their known headquarters. Each was usually an expert gunman and exceptionally fast on the draw, although frequently they did not use guns as primary weapons. Knives were also a favorite means, especially for close work and many carried large, extremely sharp "man killers" sometimes tucked in the belt, but often carried in one boot. Even among this unique class, however, there was a "pecking" order. The Chiefs' ability (and reputation) was determined by the quality and status of their respective home base saloons and as they practiced their brutal proficiency they would "graduate" upwards to a better saloon. The people and the community leaders commonly tolerated these ruffians since they seldom molested miners and other respectable citizens, but preyed on drifters, drunks, lesser criminals or each other.

The Chief was distinctly a product of the rough circumstances and the extreme remoteness of the Nevada camps; the mining camps of California during this period or even before did not have these creatures. In fact, the California gold camps were virtually tame in relation to the wild towns of the Great Basin. By 1866 most of these "bad men" had disappeared and had been replaced by stage robbers, bandits and highwaymen. The Chief killed for the love of killing, especially as an act of simple brutality. He was engulfed in a sort of play of self-deluded pride, position and reputation. The chief was foremost a performer and a psychological misfit who used mayhem and blood as a means of compensating for basic character faults. He was a very definite and clearly cut personality in the evolution of a type of civilization then developing in that rugged and uncertain land.

There were a number of such chiefs rampaging the Nevada Territory during that period. As might be expected, most were localized in the Virginia City area; lessor "quality" desperados were sometimes found in outlying camps as well. Chief among the big chiefs were Tom Peasley, Farmer Peel, Sam Brown and Jack Williams, all operating in and around Virginia City from 1860 to about 1865. Of possible chief status, were Morgan Courtney of Pioche and Oliver Roberts of several lesser known towns along the Nevada-California border, altho neither were really in the league of the established "Big" Virginia Chiefs.

Sam Brown:

The earliest and worst by far of all the early Comstock chiefs was Sam Brown. Of medium height, heavy set with a florid complexion to match, with coarse, unkempt red hair and whiskers, (which were tied under his chin), he was a fearsome sight. He wore long Spanish spurs and always had a huge Bowie knife stuck in his belt. He was a brute; slow, slovenly, repulsive and loathsome.[1] He is said to have killed many in his short career, but the known record shows only three. First, one in Texas, then in 1853, he killed a man named Lyons in Mariposa (California) and in 1854 he is known to have done in three chilenos while defending his bank. There were really more than that; there was for instance this item from the Mariposa (California) paper:

> "We are sorry to inform our readers that we have only one murder to present this week. A man named Gray was shot by a man named "long haired" Brown at Carson Creek near Aqua Fria and is not expected to recover. The difficulty originated over a game of cards. Both are gamblers. Brown struck Gray with a revolver, then shot him and fled."

This was our Sam. Whether it was due to the chilenos or the man named Gray, Sam Brown spent the next two years in San Quentin where he apparently learned little. Sam then wantonly killed a bystander in a saloon on the Hangtown Road near Coloma, California. "This thief and bully was lucky when the law and a clever lawyer managed to save him from the rope," was the resultant commentary.

He came to the Washoe Territory in the fall of 1859, spending that winter in Genoa. From the spring of 1860 until his death he divided his time and depredations between Virginia City and Carson City. Sam Brown intended from the first to be the "chief" of the area and he was. Beginning in the spring of 1860 he started his famous "man for breakfast." The first was early in March when he shot a man in Carson City, then on March 14 he became involved in a dispute with a dealer of a monte game in Virginia City. Sam drew his revolvers which were caught by his intended victim and went off, wounding two bystanders. On May 18th Brown killed "French" Pete said to be also a refugee from San Quentin. Evidently they were both gambling in a saloon in Virginia City when an old grudge between the two surfaced. Pete drew first and threatened to shoot Brown, but Brown didn't threaten. He just shot Pete—once in the head and once in the body. Pete died instantly. "No notice was taken of the affair," was the only comment of the San Francisco, (California) *Bulletin* reporting the act.

---

1) He was a big chief and when he walked into a saloon a side at a time, with his big Spanish spurs clanking along the floor and his six shooter flapping under his coat tails, the little chiefs hunted their holes and talked small in back seats." (Dan de Quille).

Then later in May, (still 1860) the following news item appeared:

Virginia City—UT, May 25, 1860

"A man of the name of Homer Woodruff died during last night from a wound received at the hands of Sam Brown, the renowned shooter and stabber. Woodruff was from Vermont, had been sober since Christmas, until a few days ago when, getting on a bender, he is said to have gone around rather courting a difficulty. At length he talked with Sam Brown and one may say used opprobrious epithets toward him and attempted to draw his revolver. Whereupon Sam very quietly and in the most gentlemanly way in the world thrust his Bowie knife into Woodruff's abdomen, gave it a turn or two "Maltese fashion" to make it sure and walked away, well satisfied, the hero of two murders and two other wounded men's misfortunes, all within two months. Woodruff was taken away and Sam Brown had the imprudence, within one half hour to visit the place wither he had been taken. The wounded man lingered on a day or two and died. His friends say he gave Brown no cause whatever for the murderous thrust. Woodruff was buried this evening and some of those present were seen nervously taking hold of their revolvers. Sam Brown left with a carpet sack this afternoon, perhaps to kill his next victim in Carson, having already a graveyard of his own at Genoa and another at Virginia City. There are no courts here, murderers have found their Eden. Brown is said to have, by the murder of Woodruff, made the number of his victims to be eight."

Brown, like all essential cowards, never bothered anyone who could and would fight back. He avoided potential victims who were either armed or had numerous friends. This is clearly illustrated in a subsequent foray, when his victim was a Bill Balboa, a loner and misfit, who Brown found late one evening, leaning against the bar in one of the many saloons along C Street in Virginia City. Brown deliberately started a quarrel with him, then stabbed him again and again.

One day, one of the boys dropped into the station Brown sometimes kept on the Carson River and indicating that he was hungry, asked for something to eat. Sam pointed to a slab of bacon hanging from the rafters and told him to help himself. "Where's your knife?" asked the man; with an odd smile Sam pulled out a large Bowie knife from his bootleg, whetted it and said, "I've killed five men with that knife and am superstitious about lending it to cut bacon."

One night early in 1861, Sam Brown felt it necessary to prove again his now secure claim to being a "big chief." The opportunity came in a C Street saloon when a weak pale-faced bar room loafer inadvertently lurched against him with a remark Brown took to be offensive. Without a word, Sam wound his gorilla-like arm around the victim's neck, drew his pallid face to his and holding him tightly, sank his Bowie knife into the man's body; the last time twisting it to completely carve the heart out. Then, flinging the bleeding body to the floor, he wiped his knife on a bar room towel and rolling up in a blanket went to sleep beside the corpse. When bystanders a few minutes later removed the body, Sam was observed to be "sleeping calmly as a child." That established his reputation for good and from then on he conducted a veritable orgy of crime. He shot men down with impunity and without provocation and no police officer seemed anxious to do anything about it. He swaggered into saloons all over the area, safe in the knowledge that he was above the law and inviolate. Sam continued this general deportment for the next several years.

In early July, 1865, he heard that one of his cronies was standing trial in Genoa in the Territorial Courtroom. Sam announced that he would ride down there, terrorize the County and have his friend released immediately on the basis of his testimony. When he entered the courtroom, his very appearance caused considerable consternation to everyone there. The Judge visibly paled, the Jury sat frozen and some of the spectators jumped from the windows or hid beneath benches expecting the worst. The only calm man in the room was Senator William Stewart, assisting the District Attorney in the prosecution of the case. Seeing the effect of the entrance and realizing what it would mean, before Brown could make a move, Stewart covered him with two Colt revolvers and ordered him to "throw up his hands." Brown, slightly alarmed at this unexpected resistance, obeyed and Stewart then ordered him to the witness stand where he was duly sworn in. "Now, Mr. Brown", Stewart said calmly, "You bragged that you could come in here and swear this defendant free and make the court accept your testimony. I am here to tell you that if you attempt any of your gun play here or give any false testimony, I will blow your fool brains out." Then Stewart, still covering him closely with his guns, made Brown admit that he not only knew nothing of the case in question, but also that the defendant had a bad reputation. By the time Stewart was finished with him, he made almost a good state's witness out of the bully. When charged with "intimidating the witness" Stewart insisted that he was merely preventing the witness from intimidating other people and then asked the witness if he felt that he was being intimidated. Brown, who had constantly bullied the entire region and whose name was feared by all who knew or had heard of him, was loath to admit this and finally managed to free himself from the growing embarrassing position by stating that he himself was under indictment in Plumas County for assault with a deadly weapon and, needing the services of a good attorney, had come to Genoa to find one. Rising from the chair, he offered Stewart $500 as a retainer to act on his behalf (which Stewart accepted). Brown then asked the court to adjourn while he "treated everyone in sight." It being late in the afternoon anyhow, the court was only too willing to adjourn to take advantage of such an offer and did so with unaccustomed alacrity. Brown, apparently in a good humor, treated the entire crowd, mounted his horse and rode away in the company of a man named Henderson. The two stopped at Webster's Hotel and sought a quarrel with Mr. Webster, but finding him ready for business and not taking any bullying they backed down and went on. A few miles south of Genoa, Henry Van Sickle, a Genoa rancher, kept a wayside station. Van Sickle was no pushover. He was an old Indian fighter, former teamster of freight wagons during the California gold rush and always kept a loaded Remington 45 cap and ball pistol conveniently handy behind the bar. Brown frequently had stopped at Van Sickle station and was well known to Van Sickle, but he usually behaved well and Van Sickle never feared him. As Brown and Henderson rode up to Van Sickle's station and the Dutchman stepped out to put up his horse, Brown said gruffly, "Now, you S. O. B., I have come to kill you" and drew his gun. Van Sickle, fully aware of Brown's character and disposition, fled, Brown following closely behind. Van Sickle ran through the dining room where some 20 men were eating supper; Brown seeing them bellowed, "Where is that S. O. B.?" But then dropped his gun and remounting rode off with his younger companion. He didn't count on the character of Van Sickle. The innkeeper had finally had enough. Van Sickle secured his double barreled shotgun, mounted, and at once pursued the two, overtaking them about three fourths of a mile from the house. When in shooting range, he called to Henderson to look out, then took a shot at Brown, missing him due to the extreme range. Brown returned the fire, ineffectively, whereupon Van Sickle shot again, taking Brown's hat off and searing his face, but not inflicting a fatal wound. Brown then spurred his horse and rode off at a furious pace. Van Sickle calmly reloaded and took out after him again, catching him some three miles further south along the trail. Once more he "turned loose." Again, Brown returned the fire, but neither had any effect. Again Brown rode off with Van Sickle following with an empty gun. Brown then reached W. Cosser's house where he took refuge. By now several persons were following Van Sickle and knowing that he had only two charges for his shotgun, brought fresh ammunition. After reloading Van Sickle watched the house closely and Brown finally came out to make another attempt to run. By now it was getting dark and Brown was in a cold terror, realizing that here finally was a man capable and fully determined to kill him. At dusk Brown reached the Mott residence (Mottsville) and leaping from his horse he begged Mrs. Mott to protect him. Brown got inside the house just as Van Sickle rode up. Van Sickle waited for him to come out, but Brown sneaked out the back door and disappeared in the darkness. Van Sickle finally entreated a passerby to enter the house to see what Brown was doing; when he found that Brown was gone, Van Sickle immediately headed for Luther Olds Hotel expecting to find him there. He was not there, but Van Sickle still thought he would come, so he sat down to wait. In about a half an hour, a horse was heard in the darkness and as Brown dismounted, Van Sickle stepped out at short range and covered him. With a scream of terror, Brown begged for his life, but Van Sickle said, "You S. O. B., I have got you now," discharged both barrels, blowing the top of Brown's head off. Death was immediate.

This all happened on the 6th of July, 1865; on the 8th the jury brought in a verdict that Sam Brown had come to his death by a "just dispensation of an all wise Providence." Van Sickle was fully exonerated and the general valley reaction was that Brown's death "served him right." Brown was buried at Van Sickle's expense, but there were no mourners.

Langford (Farmer) Peel:

He was quite definitely one of the "chiefs" of the time, but he was comparatively unknown beyond the Virginia City outskirts. He was feared, second only to the notorious Sam Brown, but in many ways he was even more dangerous, particularly since he did not look the part. He was believed to be originally from Liverpool and a relative of Sir Robert Peel, the originator of the London Police Force, although this is not certain. He served time in the cavalry and learned to kill in the various Indian wars. He also spent some time in the South, but came to Virginia Town from Salt Lake City. He then had a reported six known murders to his credit and as it was said, at least five more unknown; within a year or two he added many more.

He was never the aggressor in these fights, but always was efficient and successful. His first fight (and very nearly his last) was in Salt Lake City. He was broke and sought to borrow $50 from a Faro dealer in order to "buck the game." This request was of course refused and it so infuriated Peel that he began to beat the dealer over the head with his own apparatus, finally driving him from the room. The gambler then returned with a gun which he fired at Peel, wounding him seriously. To most men, it would have been a fatal shot, but Peel, before he fell, managed to draw his gun, fire and kill his attacker.

Among most old time desperados there was a strong belief that some men have such tenacity to life that they can't be killed. Peel was such a believer and in fact held to it with such implicitness that it gave him extreme confidence and made others fear him all the more. "Someone may get me from behind when I am not looking," he often boasted, "but I'll get him before I drop." This first killing really started him on the path to becoming a known and recognized killer. Soon after, still in Salt Lake City, he became involved one night in a bar room quarrel with a soldier. Both had emptied their guns at each other and both fell wounded to the floor. Peel, while lying here bleeding and, as he thought, mortally wounded, drew his Bowie knife and crawling painfully over to the inert body of the soldier, stabbed him in the heart. This established his reputation far and wide and when he moved on to the then infant camp on Sun Mountain,[2] he was accorded all the respect and deference usually observed for such men of his proven caliber.

Peel was a decidedly singular person. Only of medium height and of slight build, he was nevertheless of manly proportions and possessed great strength and dignity, was always courteous and gracious and exhibited a sort of "noble presence," characteristic of the gentry from the southern states. He sported a golden beard and manners so pleasant and unassuming that some actually thought him soft. He was never boisterous, drank politely and, all in all, behaved in so attractive a manner that the rumor was circulated up and down "C" Street that he was a graduate of Harvard University, although there is no record of this. When sober he was mild and as agreeable a gentlemen as was to be found anywhere on Montgomery Street in San Francisco, but when he was drunk he became a veritable demon—a monster and one not to be trifled with. But either way he was still an uncontrollable killer since a killer is dependent on instinct, a pure reaction, without thinking, a subconscious reflex that never sleeps and never gets drunk. That did not mean that he was quarrelsome as he never actually hunted a fight, but he had earned the title of "chief" and he was always ready to defend it. Peel shot from the hip and his aim was deadly. "The secret of shooting," he once proclaimed, "is to shoot first." He followed this advice himself and to the end his motto was always: "Do unto others as they would do to you, but do it first."

Dick Paddock, another of the well known tough men on the Comstock, accosted him one day in a saloon and began a petty quarrel of some kind. Peel tolerated Paddock's abuse for some time, but said nothing. A few months later, Paddock, meeting him again and thinking him reluctant, challenged him with "Do you want to take it up?" "I haven't any objections," said Peel in his usual quiet way. "Very well," said Peel and after they had taken their positions and opened fire, Paddock lay disabled on the ground with a wound in his chest and right hand while Peel was unhurt. Paddock recovered and was later killed in Virginia City on January 2, 1877, by Thomas Hughes in a saloon row.

The killing for which Farmer Peel was best known, however, was that of El Dorado Johnny or "Austin Johnny," who had a reputation of sorts in Austin and some of the eastern Nevada camps as a hellion.[3] He was a little Irishman, fresh in town, who fancied himself a chief, although he was anything but the type. It was said that his real name was John Dennis, but for some reason

---

2) Virginia City.
3) Not the fighting or "Austin" Johnny, whose real name was John Doyle, a Denver rough from Pioche, Eureka and Reno, who came to Virginia City in 1875 and within a year was arrested 10 times for drinking and fighting.

everywhere on the Comstock he was known only as "El Dorado," and that is the name that appears on his headstone. Johnny decided that one chief was enough for the area and decided to kill Peel or be killed in the process. Johnny asked a friend, George Birdsall, to introduce him to Peel. Birdsall tried to dissuade him, telling him of Peel's prowess as a gunfighter and accuracy as a marksman. "Why, Johnny," said Birdsall, "Peel can put all six balls from his gun into a circle an inch in diameter without lowering his arm and flip a dime into the air and hit it before it reaches the ground." Johnny replied, "I tell you I'm going to take the scalp of this bully boy or he's going to take mine." "Well Johnny, your scalp will be the one taken if you run against Peel." "Well," said Johnny, "If I'm going to die with my boots on, I guess I better have them polished." The two went to Ben Irwin's Saloon where they found Peel drinking with the boys. George introduced the two killers. Johnny asked Peel and friends to drink with him and then addressing Peel said, "Mr. Peel, you are the chief over this here neck of the woods and I am chief of the rest of the world. There is not room on this world for two chiefs, so one of us has got to pass in his chips." "Why, my friend," said Peel, "I have no desire to be chief anywhere or of anything. I am one who never seeks trouble. It is true I have been compelled to defend my life against the attacks of desperate men, but I have never been the aggressor and it has been to me a source of sorrow that I was ever forced to take the life of a fellow man. Have a drink, shake hands and be friends." "This talk of yours, Peel, don't cut any ice with me, I'll tell you," said Johnny putting his hand on his gun, "That one of us two has got to die." "Well," said Peel, "If nothing will satisfy you, but to gun play with me, don't let us pull it off here. This room is too crowded with people who have no part or parcel in this affair and maybe one or more might be hurt or killed. Let us go out to the street where the life of no one else will be endangered." Johnny sidled backwards through the saloon toward the door with Peel close behind. When Johnny reached the opposite side of the street, he squatted and was taking careful aim with the pistol over his left arm, when Peel standing in the doorway of the saloon, shot Johnny squarely between the eyes killing him instantly.

Several bystanders carried the body to the saloon. Peel turned and said to Birdsall, "George, what in the name of all that is evil, made you bring that boy here to have trouble with me? You surely knew that he had no chance to win out in a game like that with me and you should have kept him away." "Farmer," said Birdsall, "I did all I could and used every argument I could think of to prevent his coming, but it did no good." "Oh, well," said Peel "It can't be helped now, but I am very sorry that it happened. That poor fellow knew nothing about handling a gun and it was like shooting a baby, but what could I do? He had his gun trained on me and had it gone off, my body instead of his, might be lying there and I almost wish it was. George, you go up to Brown's and tell him to come and prepare the body for burial. Tell him to spare no expense, but to give him the best he has in the shop and I will pay for everything." Brown, the undertaker dressed the body in fine robes with a magnificent casket, which lay in state from Friday to Sunday in the same saloon. Seven bartenders were busy handling refreshments for thirsty hundreds who visited the place and the remains were escorted to the cemetery with a huge procession. The doors of all the saloons in Virginia City were draped in mourning and everything was closed. An air of sadness pervaded the town, while the band played mournful music. Pete Larkin, another gunman, later hung for murder, was the master of ceremonies at the grave. He gave a great speech. The people returned to town to the tune "When Johnny Came Marching Home."

El Dorado, for a relative newcomer in camp, had a surprising number of friends and during the next few months, five of them tried individually to take Peel. All five ended in the boot hill below camp.

Peel was never punished for his killings, in fact he was not even arrested. The local police were far from anxious to meddle with so deadly an adversary, especially since most of his depredations involved the less wanted element of the population. Consequently, most, if not all, of his actions went unchecked. One day he got gloriously drunk and raised so much trouble that there was a general ultimatum from the public for his arrest. Peel defied and killed the deputy who served the summons. He dared the law to come and get him, adding he could be found anytime in the Ophir Saloon. The challenge became a public issue; meetings were held in other saloons where citizens determined to take steps to rectify the problem once and for all. There was also a meeting at the Ophir, but for a different reason. On trial morning, Judge Davenport apprehended Peel at the bar in the Ophir. "Come to Court, Peel," he said, "The State wants the likes of you." The Judge was a small man with a white beard of which he was quite proud. Peel, pretending fear, followed him willingly to Court, where he leaned up against the rail, smiling at his friends, while the bailiff proclaimed the session. The entire town was surprised and shocked that Peel was there and many crowded into the small room. The Judge demanded order, got it and asked if the defendant had counsel. "What was that?" Peel wanted to know. When it was explained, Peel said he did not need a lawyer to settle his troubles. "I'll do my own work here," he said and with that Peel seized the Judge by his long side whiskers with both hands and pounded his head against the desk until the befuddled man was nearly unconscious, finally letting him drop, a shapeless heap, to the floor. He then turned, surveyed the half dozen assorted police officers standing around the room as if rooted to the spot and calmly walked out of the door. Some laughed, but most kept their eyes away as Peel strode from the room, black coat open and his hand on the handle of his gun. This was the last of the affair as far as any of the authorities were concerned and, needless to say, no fine was ever collected or was it ever mentioned again. Peel never paid fines anyway and no one dared either to remind him or try to collect, but most chiefs were rather obliging about paying fines; in fact, they paid cheerfully as sort of a bounty for the act of murder. Sugarfoot Jack, another local chief, reported to court immediately after killing a man (a desperado named Robinson) to confess the deed. He testified that Robinson had drawn first, that he killed him, not only in self defense, but because he was not certain Robinson was such a good shot that he would miss a miner standing nearby having a beer. So Sugarfoot paid his fine and received the congratulations of the court for acting in such a public purpose.

In the winter of 1866, Peel left Virginia City, never to return. He first drifted to Belmont in Nye County, but left in May of the following year for Montana. A prospector, John Bull, went to Helena with him. They were interested in silver possibilities in the hills around the Last Chance Gulch. In July, 1867, Bull came into town with ore so poor that Peel flew into a rage, accusing Bull of "trifling with him." A quarrel soon developed and Peel drew his gun. "I'm not heeled," said Bull. "Go heel yourself then," roared Peel, slapping Bull across the face. Bull, now thoroughly aroused, armed himself and returned. Next door to the saloon where Peel was drinking down his wrath, was a store in front of which were piled many dry good cases. Bull hid himself behind the boxes and waited. When Peel finally came out, Bull, with no warning, fired the first bullet, dropping him instantly. As Peel fell, Bull jumped from cover and bending over the prostrate Peel, pumped the rest of the bullets into his body. Bull was tried for murder, but the jury disagreed and a new trial was ordered. In the meantime Bull left town and since no one was interested enough to go after him—no trial was held and the entire matter was soon forgotten. Peel died July 23, 1867, at the age of 36 and he was buried in the cemetery in Helena. On his tombstone appears the following words: "Vengeance is mine sayeth the Lord."

Reflections of crystal chandeliers in the mirror of the Old Washoe Club, Virginia City.
This was the most elite establishment of them all. Its membership was limited to millionaires only.
The "Chiefs" were not of this class.

Tom Peasley:

Peasley was an enigma and an anomaly. He was 32 when he arrived on the Comstock in 1860. Tall, compactly built and of exceptional strength, he was also quick and agile in action and decision. He was perfectly coordinated and a natural leader, although his lack of education prevented him from becoming the born leader he might otherwise have become. Accordingly he was content to lead his own class. His animal spirits, complemented by his immense strength, together with a certain tendency for strong spirits and a quick temper, frequently led him into dangerous paths. The realization that he was a "chief" and something daring and provocative was expected of him only strengthened his temperance behavior, but Peasley was more of a leader than a killer. His claim to the title "chief" was based on leadership merit rather than pure terror (as was the case of Brown). He is said to have been involved in many other scrapes, but the record is silent as to actual killings.

He soon found the drudgery of working underground in the mines distasteful; he craved excitement and activity and he found it in fighting fires, which were plentiful in this wooden town. He established himself in the Old Sazerac Saloon on C Street near Union, which immediately became the headquarters for firemen and a concomitant attraction for all political aspirants seeking this group's support. He gathered a number of ex-firemen around him and from this enthusiasm grew a voluntary fire committee which eventually led to the development of Virginia Engine Company No. 1. Peasley was elected foreman. Subsequently, when the Virginia City Hook and Ladder Company No. 1 was organized, Peasley was elected foreman of that also. When five or six rival companies were created, he became Chief Engineer of all of them.

At first the Virginia City Engine Company had the most powerful apparatus on the Pacific coast. Peasley ordered it in New York. It featured a 9-1/4" cylinder, a 7-1/2" stroke and 24' brakes with 600 feet of hose. When the younger rival Engine Company No. 2 ordered an engine with 10" cylinders and a hose that could throw five streams at the same time, trouble began brewing. Peasley had 64 men under him, big powerful men, all generally happy-go-lucky, but terrible when aroused. All were Union men, all leaders and important personages in the community. With control of the engine companies, Peasley began to bring the energetic (but often aimless) reckless elements in town under a form of control; they had to conform to regulations, toe the line or not be a member of the Engine Company, which was by then of great prestige and a much sought after status. After the entire company was established on a firm basis, he collected funds and built the engine house on C Street, which soon developed into the most powerful political unit on the lode, with Peasley in overall command.

With a power base similar to Tammany Hall, it established him as the main political force in town. Then Peasley divided the town into four wards, built a tall red fire tower high on the mountain and established a 24 hour watch to warn the city if fire should break out. This eventually led to his election as Sheriff from 1862 to 1864 (one wonders how he tolerated Sam Brown operating in the same area at the same time).

Sometimes Peasley's giant strength was a cause of difficulty; to knock a friend down with a playful slap on the back was his usual form of greeting, and to break a door down instead of unlocking it only indicated he was on a particular intimacy with the occupant. Once when in such a mood, he met Langford Peel in front of the International Hotel and banged his head against the wall for no other reason than he didn't like chiefs. Why he was not killed for that one no one knows, but Tom was a pretty rough boy and Peel knew it.

One of the many youths who affected toughness and sought the exciting life on the Comstock at this time was one known only as "Sugarfoot Jack." (Jack Jenkins) He hadn't a single qualification for the title "desperado" except the ambition to be one. At a masquerade ball held in September of 1863, Peasley knocked him down in an excess of rough playfulness. This affront would be too much for a true tough who would have resented it on the spot, but not Jack. He left the ballroom muttering threats and proclaiming his intent to "get" Peasley. Some of Peasley's friends informed him of Jack's intent and that he had armed himself and was laying for him. The counter hunt began immediately. Sugarfoot was discovered "hiding" behind an awning post, in front of the Niagara Hall on North B Street, a position of decidedly no advantage or defense.

Peasley drew and riddled the boy, who had, at last, fulfilled his ambition to "die with his boots on." Peasley was indicted for Second Degree Murder, but was found not guilty at a trial held January 7, 1865 (A decision that took less than five minutes). The threats and actions of Sugarfoot plainly made it self-defense, but that somehow changed Peasley. He was no longer so boisterous and he withdrew from the saloon business and went into "theatrical management" at McQuire's Opera House.

During the winter of 1864-1865, Peasley, then Sergeant at Arms of the State Senate, and his deputy, Edward Connelly, were sitting by the stove in the Ormsby House Saloon in Carson City, drinking and talking with some friends; all were slightly tipsy. A man named Squires (later in the State Prison for nine years for arson) came in. Peasley asked a friend who he was and when told Squires was an ardent secessionist became enraged and said he would "whip Squires that night." A few moments later he turned from the bar and saw a man named Barnhart standing by the stove. Mistaking him for Squires he knocked him in the face. Barnhart drew his gun, but before he could fire, it either slipped or was knocked from his hand to the floor. Peasley having drawn also, fired two or three shots, the balls striking the buckle on Barnhart's belt and deflecting. They did no damage except a slight flesh wound. At this point the bystanders interfered and the matter ended, at least that is what Peasley thought. Peasley and Connelly were both arrested, Connelly fined and Peasley discharged. Peasley and Barnhart were strangers to each other and as soon as Peasley was released he hunted for Barnhart, to explain to him the mistake, to apologize to the young man and offer reparations. Barnhart rebuffed these and nursed a hidden resentment. During the following summer while both were at Glenbrook at Lake Tahoe, Barnhart sent a challenge to Peasley to fight with him with pistols; Peasley declined saying he didn't want to add further harm to the injury he so sincerely regretted. This didn't satisfy Barnhart who now thought Peasley was afraid of him.

The following winter on February 1, 1866, Peasley was again in Carson City to visit some old friends from the Legislature. He and Ned Ingham were playing billiards at Sawyer's Saloon when they saw Barnhart and two companions come in, take several drinks and leave. About 2 A.M. Peasley was in the Ormsby House Saloon and sitting near the stove talking with John C. Lewis, proprietor of the Eastern Slope (a newspaper of Washoe City), and John Benham of Virginia City. These two gentlemen were on either side of Peasley. Barnhart and a friend, named Charley Moore, who recently had arrived from Austin, came in, went to the bar and had several more drinks. Barnhart then went over to Peasley and said, "Tom, why did you not fight with me at Glenbrook House last summer?" Peasley, not understanding, replied "Good evening" (or something similar), whereupon Barnhart repeated the question. Peasley asked "Are you always on the fight?" Barnhart replied, "Yes, you son of a bitch, and I will give it to you now," immediately drawing his pistol and firing point blank at Peasley, the ball entered Peasley's breast; the second shot also in the chest. At the second shot, Peasley started to rise from his chair, but Barnhart began to beat him over the head with the pistol until he broke the pivot on which the chamber revolved and the barrel fell to the floor, leaving only the handle in Barnhart's hand. Peasley, now helpless, called out, "Don't let him murder me. What are you all doing?" Peasley had now revived somewhat, staggered to his feet and with a strong effort he seized Barnhart by the collar of his coat and threw him through a light sash door into a adjoining dark room. Peasley drew his gun and fired three shots—two shots taking effect on the prostrate Barnhart, one through the heart and the other through the thigh. (He was killed instantly). Peasley tried to empty his gun, but the chamber would not revolve and jammed. He fell backwards on the floor exclaiming "By, God, I'm shot through and through." He was taken upstairs to the billiard room and laid on the table. He managed to speak some few words in a whisper, asking for his brother in Gold Hill, for something to relieve the pain and to take his boots off, which were done.

Both were muscular men. Peasley after being shot through and through the body and his head crushed, still had enough vitality to stand, seize Barnhart and throw him down, then draw and shoot him twice.

The death of Peasley was a tremendous shock to the people of Virginia City. The body lay in state for a full day and all of the fire brigades of Virginia City staged a funeral demonstration which has yet to be matched. The body was shipped to San Francisco for burial.

The friends of Barnhart also conducted a large funeral.

The Carson City coroner's report said it all: "Upon our oaths, we each and all do say that we find the deceased, Thomas Peasley, was a native of New York, age about 38 years, and that he came to his death on the second day of February, 1866, in this city, by pistol shots fired by Martin V. Barnhart, in the Ormsby House and at the time aforesaid, we also find that the said Martin V. Barnhart was a native of Indiana, aged about 24 years, that he came to his death on the second day of February, 1866, by pistol shots fired by Thomas Peasley at the Ormsby House and at the time aforesaid. We further find that each killed each other intentionally."

Jack Williams:

The first public notice of Jack Williams occurred in the winter of 1860-61 in Virginia City where he "assumed" the title and functions of night watchman. There was no authority for such at that time, but he took the duties by "common consent" (without protest) and he wielded an authority based entirely on terror. Williams was a native of Britain, of medium stature, but with an enormous head and large shoulders, which indicated his immense strength. He was prone to boast of his ability with a gun, often illustrating this by striking his cocked gun in the face of the listener or flourishing it over his head "usually scaring the hell out of them." He soon began to think of himself as a chief and especially when unchallenged.

Billy Brown (a common gambler) was the first to question his claim. In the spring of 1861 in the Washoe Saloon on North C Street at 11:00 P.M. on a bitterly cold night (as only the high desert can produce), he sat watching a game of billiards. Brown, after some considerable drinking finally noticed Williams across the room and told him to "draw out and defend himself" while drawing his gun from his belt. Williams sprang to the side of the billiard table opposite Billy and as Brown levelled his gun, Williams crouched under the table. Brown fired, the ball striking the table, then glancing upwards. Before he could fire again, Williams rose and sent a bullet through Brown's heart, killing him instantly. The plea was of course "self defense" (which was obvious) and Williams was not charged or held.

Williams was now a full fledged "chief" and obliged to meet all comers. A few months later he became involved in a scrap with a Jack (Sailor) Baird, a dangerous character. Jack was only slightly wounded in the affair and was later killed by his Spanish mistress.

Comstockers now began to avoid him at all costs; no one affronted him openly. One night he was discovered, while on "duty" in the commitment of an act of highway robbery. Actually this had been going on for some time, but no one deemed it prudent to mention it, much less initiate an investigation. He was not arrested for this (everyone was afraid!), but he was excused from the police force. Then he became totally and utterly reckless and degenerate. He became a grim, swaggering, red-eyed bully, living off the terror of restaurateurs, of the saloon keepers and gambling houses. He would never pay for meals or drink, sat himself at any table, appropriating what chips he wished from the dealers or other players stacks, and generally acted as he pleased, totally unmolested.

Finally the town decided it had to end. One December night in 1862 while Williams was playing 21 in the back of Lynch's B Street Saloon, three men (all of whose records were almost equally bad) shook dice in front of the same bar to decide which one would kill him. Joe McGee, as reptilian an assassin as ever disgraced the region "won" the contest.

McGee borrowed a shotgun, stationed himself outside the rear door of the saloon, while one of the confederates fired his gun in the front door of the bar. During the resulting melee to ascertain what had taken place, McGee opened the rear door a crack, thrust the gun through and poured both barrels at a six-foot range into Williams neck and chest. Williams fell, 19 buckshot in his chest within a hand's space. No one paid any attention other than some who looked curiously at the wound. The body lay there uncovered all night and half the next day. No one saw McGee fire and it was some time before it was known who had done the deed.

McGee hung around Virginia City for about a year, but begun to worry, developed a case of poor health and was always ill. He felt it prudent to leave the Comstock so he went to Carson City to catch the stage to California. The stage was not due until 2:30 P.M. McGee sat in the Ormsby House by the bar waiting and smoking a cigar. A charge of buckshot fired through a window dropped him instantly and he died without knowing who was the killer. The killer was John Daley, also a cutthroat and desperado, who was hung in Aurora a few months later by vigilantes.

Hank Parris:

He would probably be classified as only a minor "tough," but he was a major problem of his day. Not a great deal is known of his early life, but supposedly he began his career in Wyoming and Idaho where he acquired a reputation for being "mean, vile tempered and decidedly anti-social in temperament." In 1870, Parris turned up in El Dorado, a remote camp in the southern desert, only 39 miles from Las Vegas.[4] He became associated there in a mining venture with a man named Paddock. One evening during a card game in one of the local saloons, Parrish, who was

---

4) El Dorado was originally Indian workings until about 1857 when some placer operations began. This Later turned to silver and the camp began to be quite attractive to San Francisco investors even though it was very remote and difficult to reach or supply. It was then part of the Arizona Territory, but in 1867 it became a part of Nevada. In the early years it was a tough and lawless camp. The nearest Law was the Sheriff of Lincoln County in Hiko (before 1871) or in Pioche (after 1871). It was 200 miles of dubious roads, extremely difficult terrain and uncertain Indians; generally not worth the effort for the various affrays in El Dorado. After 1905, the town was moved some seven miles west to El Dorado Canyon and renamed Nelson. The original site is now under the waters of Lake Mohave.

somewhat drunk, called his partner a "cheat" and went for his gun. The bystanders, well used to the signs of this action, scattered. Parrish's shot only wounded Paddock in the leg. Paddock mounted his horse and rode off into the desert. Parrish, enraged at his escape, borrowed a horse (without asking), and rode furiously in pursuit of Paddock. He soon overtook him and finished his original intent, leaving the body in the open desert. For some reason he was not persecuted for this cold blooded murder, but feelings were high in El Dorado, so he moved on to the Kiel Ranch in Las Vegas Valley, a locale not especially noted for its law-abiding attitude nor its desire to live peaceably with nearby citizens and neighbors. While at the Kiel Ranch he was implicated in a murder there of an Archibald Stewart, although no proof was presented that he was actually involved and he was not named as a defendant in the subsequent trial.

Three years later in about 1884, he arrived at Pioche, where he joined the "Army" of incorrigibles who were terrorizing the town, high-grading whenever and wherever possible and in general contributing to the unbridled lawlessness so characteristic of that time. In 1890 his welcome finally grew thin in Pioche and Parrish moved to Royal City[5] in Lincoln County not far from Pioche.

Shortly after his arrival he was, one evening, a very drunk bystander and audience at a local poker game being conducted in the rear of the local saloon. Due to his inebriated condition and the rumors that had preceded him he was not asked to join in the card game, a rejection which galled him considerably and led to some scuffling and jousting with the other bystanders. One of these politely asked Parrish to "stand back and not to bother the players," at which Parrish responded with a stream of oaths. Pete Thompson, a bystander, told him to shut his mouth; Parrish instantly drew his Bowie knife and stabbed Thompson inflicting fatal wounds. Thompson's friends immediately disarmed Parrish and pinned him to the floor.

Local sentiment was strongly in favor of lynching, but the sheriff of Lincoln County was called and Parrish was soon in jail in Pioche. It was patently obvious that feelings in Pioche were highly inflamed against Parrish and that it would be impossible to impanel a jury of uncommitted and impartial men. The trial was, therefore, moved to nearby White Pine County and in short order a verdict of guilty was duly carried out on 11 December, 1890 in Ely. Parrish, at the gallows, delivered a short speech blaming all his troubles on a "short temper and evil companions."

5) Royal City, later renamed Jackrabbit, northwest of Pioche. Silver ore was located here on the east slope of the Bristol Range in 1876. Within months there was a saloon, store, blacksmith and restaurant. In 1891, a 15 mile narrow gauge railroad, the "Jackrabbit Road" connected the mines at Royal to the smelter at Pioche. The railroad named their station "Jackrabbit Road," which soon superseded the older name.

ELEVEN

SOME EARLY DAY SALOON TOUGHS

The mining towns of early Nevada had a fair share of other characters who generally distinguished themselves with varying forms of anti-social behavior, most often directly or indirectly associated with the plethora of saloons available. Most were simply bullies, ruffians, (often drunk or nearly so,) always belligerent and sometimes prone to violence. These bullies are not to be confused with the more bloody saloon "chiefs" of an earlier period (for the most part before 1870); these bullies and roughs came after 1870, and in some cases extending to the present day.

One of these, but not the most notorious by any means, who divided his forays almost equally between Virginia City in Nevada and Bodie in California, was Mike McGowan, sometimes called "Red Mike" or the "man-eater." He originally earned his nickname in Virginia City were he was well known for biting off the ears and noses of his many victims. The fact that his head was considerably beaten out of shape indicated, however, that he didn't win all altercations he aroused. McGowan was a cook by trade and was reported to be a very good one when he was sober, but only when he was sober, which was as seldom as he could arrange. When drunk, he rapidly became the terror of each town and this soon became too often for the Christian community and their ladies to tolerate.

After a series of minor but continuous depredations in Virginia City in early 1889 he transferred his attentions from this metropolis to Bodie,[1] where he soon managed to become a major public menace there as well. He began by taking a large bite from Sheriff Taylor's leg, then chased a terrified man through the town, brandishing a large and lethal butcher knife, culminating in a threat to chew off the ears of the Justice of the Peace. In between, he ate a stray bulldog and engaged in innumerable fist fights. It finally reached a point where a select committee of stable citizens (and the law) backed him against a wall and gave him a choice of either a long term in the Bodie Jail, or permanent exile from the town and its environs forthwith. He wisely chose the latter and promptly returned to the more congenial Virginia City where he accelerated his errant deportment and was soon arrested for vagrancy. The *Bodie Standard*, on hearing of this, remarked "this must be a mistake on the part of the authorities (there) for Mike does have available a means of support. He has upper and lower rows of teeth." Mike continued his forays in Virginia City, but on a considerably diminished scale and finally disappeared from public view.

Some might be tempted to classify McGowan as a "chief" in the select company of such well known and entitled ruffians as Farmer Peel, Sam Brown, and Courtney Morgan. He hardly is in their class, however, and could not be considered more than "only a nuisance."

Another "two bit" desperado was "Two-Gun" Mike Kennedy, "one of the toughest men to come from the east." At least that is what Mike thought and he tried hard to prove it on all occasions.

---

1) In 1880, Bodie boasted a population of about 10,000, with 72 mines and mills operating 24 hours a day. There were also 64 saloons and 15 houses of prostitution. Much of the town remains today, preserved in a "state of arrested decay" as a California State Park.

Sodaville in 1904 was a pretty tough town. This site was known as Soda Springs in 1870, but was inactive until 1881, when the Carson & Colorado Railroad established a station. By 1901 it was a very busy terminal and by 1904 long lines of 20 Mule Team freight wagons were hauling loads daily to the booming outlying silver camps of Nye County, returning with cargoes of ore. But all of that ended by 1905, when the Tonopah Railroad moved the roundhouse and operations to nearby Mina. Sodaville was located on the westerly side of the Rhodes Salt Marsh in present day Mineral County, between Coaldale Junction and Hawthorne. As usual, the town wasn't much, just a collection of wooden shacks lined up on a dusty street. Most of these were liquor palaces of some sort, all of them catering to the hard working miners, teamsters and gamblers. Of these, the Hard Rock Saloon was the largest, most popular and most active, operating as usual around the clock and dispensing raw spirits, conviviality and girls, as the occasion demanded.

James Lund, a mild mannered, inoffensive and generally lackluster prospector, was in from one of the nearby "diggins" for a little fun one Saturday night, which happened to be the night that "Two-Gun" was being particularly officious. This went on for some time. Although unarmed, Lund finally called Kennedy's bluff whereupon Mike invited the innocent (and naive) miner outside to "shoot it out." Lund then borrowed a gun and the two squared off in the center of the main street outside the bar as everyone else scattered for cover, all in the basic traditional Hollywood manner. They both commenced to blaze away and when the smoke had cleared, the "toughest man ever to come out of the east" fell with six bullets in his body. Slightly bewildered by it all, but totally unharmed, James Lund went back into the saloon for many more rounds of drinks and the amazed congratulations and enthusiasm of his fellows.

"Pioche Kelly" was another of the saloon bullies of early Nevada. He was the reputed "tough" of the Bodie District and it was said that every door and every wall in his house had a mirror attached to it so that no one could attack him from the rear without warning. He was, however, really a good natured fellow when not "in the cups" and a strong supporter of the "fair deal." He came to Bodie from Pioche with an established reputation as a killer. It so happened that "Old Bill" Irwin, the general manager of the Standard Mining Company, the richest property in camp, sensed the need for a bodyguard. He was seated one morning in the barber chair when Pioche came in for a shave. "Old Bill," always alert for danger, watched closely as Pioche took off his coat revealing a huge revolver strapped to his belt. Instantly, while Irwin watched intently, it disappeared and Pioche took his seat in the chair. As the barber pulled the cloth around his neck, Irwin asked him politely, "What happened to that gun, Mister? " " It's on your heart, Mister," said Pioche, "You need a bodyguard." "You're hired," was Irwin's instant reply. Pioche was so fast on the draw it was hard to follow it. Because of this he soon became constable of the town. Charley Jardine robbed the Bodie-Hawthorne one night and got away with a fairly decent size shipment of bullion. Kelly, then a "deputy" sheriff, investigated the matter and found witnesses implicating Jardine. Jardine, hearing of this, said "He would like to see the man who could arrest him." "Well, when I get word from the coast to arrest Jardine, I will do it, " said Pioche. As fate would have it, a few hours later they met unexpectedly on the corner of Main and King Streets. Jardine pulled his gun. No one saw Pioche move, but Jardine dropped dead on the spot. Kelly hung around Pioche for awhile, then drifted away and no one knows what eventually happened to him, although it was rumored he died in bed—a most unusual and unexpected ending.

Gordon Ellis also ranked high among the famous "dead shots" of the early west. He was said to be the "quickest on the draw," often daring his victims to draw first, then moving so fast that the eye could not follow. He never missed his target but never killed anyone (since he was adverse to murder). He would only cripple them by shooting them in the leg. Ellis sold a borax claim near Death Valley and then dropped over to Pahrump Valley for a visit to Bennett's Ranch. This was a lush spring fed oasis with a popular bar, both meccas for a dusty miner. On the first day, after several hours before the plank, he became involved in an argument with a Mexican and promptly shot him in the leg (legend has it that there were many such victims in the area in those days, all easily identifiable by a limp or crutches). One the second day, following another long period of liquid enforcement, he had another argument; this time with an Irishman by the name of Pat Shea, and he also drilled him in the leg. But Shea refused to quit and from the littered barroom floor derogated Ellis in magnificent language until Ellis, enraged, shot him in the other leg and then left. Public reaction was now aroused and some local citizens blocked his path, compelling him to return to the barroom. Shea did not appreciate his reappearance, continuing to swear at Ellis, but also turning a stream of invective to a nearby bystander. This man dared Pat to stand up on his shattered legs and fight, throwing his six gun on the floor. Shea, with great difficulty, dragged himself to his feet and tottered a few steps until he reached the gun. He then picked up the weapon and cocked it. This act so unnerved Ellis that he ran for his horse hitched at the doorstep. Shea called to Ellis to come out from behind his horse. Ellis then tried a fast potshot from behind the horse hitting Shea in the groin, but he still refused to fall. Shea then shot twice, missing the first, but the second hit Ellis. Shea slumped to the ground, but again pushed himself into a sitting position. Weak from the loss of blood, he took both hands to lift the six gun to aim again. The barrel wobbled and the rest of the camp seemed to be swaying back and forth in the line of sight. He called out to them to "get out of the way" so he could get another shot at Ellis. Ellis, at the feet of his horse, heard him and called out, "Don't let him shoot, I've had enough" and died. Shea recovered, but there was no arrest and no trial. The people of Pahrump found $100.00 on Ellis' body, which was just "enough to pay for a proper burial."

Shotgun Johnny Heilshorn was a little fellow and an undertaker by trade, but he was generally known as a "Rounder by profession, thief by inclination, dope fiend by choice and a scalawag by association." He eventually drifted into Bodie (where undertakers were sorely needed) and found no trouble getting a job. He had a strange habit of abbreviating words which sometimes made him difficult to understand. A farmer came to town not long after he arrived, and after selling his load of grain, retired to a nearby stable to spend the night. He was held up by a lone robber carrying a #8 shotgun, larger than he was, and the farmer remembered that the robber had said when he found no money "The prop is to go through him again." This was enough to identify Heilshorn, however, authorities were not enough interested to arrest him. One dark night soon after he and "Big Bill" Monohan (a comrade of the same ilk) were seen coming from the cemetery carrying a coffin. The Sheriff found this same coffin in Johnny's place of business the next day and a new grave in the cemetery in which reposed a body without benefit of a coffin. Bodie, tough as it was, shuddered at the thought of using second hand coffins and Johnny's business soon died. He did too, with an overdose of morphine.

Another liquor related fracas occurred in the summer of 1905 in Silver Peak, some 25 miles southerly of present Coaldale Junction in Nye County. It has always been an isolated camp.

Surrounded by dry mountains and barren salt flats, it is the only operation within a large area. Usually it was a fairly quiet place. A gunman named Al Cook started trouble one day by kicking a dog belonging to a popular and gentlemanly man named McIvor. Bad blood soon arose, particularly since they saw each other daily and both lived on raw liquor. Cook was reputed to be a rough and rugged professional gunman from Arizona. McIvor was a slender, quiet, well-bred chap. But he was a drifter as was practically everyone else in the camp. After several days of increasing animosity the two men happened to exit two of the town's several saloons at the same time, facing each other on opposite sides of the main and only street. No one knows who went for his gun first, but in no time both men were blazing away, rocking echoes off the dusty fronts of the buildings. Cook had backed into the frame of the entrance to <u>Tom</u> <u>Carter's</u> <u>Saloon</u>, while McIvor had ducked behind the jam at the door to <u>John</u> <u>Shirley's</u> <u>Bar</u> across the street and at a protecting angle. Both men fired several shots at a close range.

And, right through the hail of bullets, happily loaded with raw Irish whiskey, waving an empty bottle and singing a popular Spanish War ballad "Good-bye, Little Girl, Good-bye...," staggered the town character known as the "Frenchman." He dipped and weaved directly through the line of fire, singing all the time, and emerging on the other end, unscratched—continued his erratic way down the main street.

Cook aimed a heavy slug through the protecting door jam and it splintered a plank, penetrating McIvor's abdomen. He slumped to the boardwalk and was carried upstairs to his room nearby. Doc Harper was summoned, but was confronted by an indignant landlady who demanded McIvor be hauled out of her place before "His blood stained the floor."

Cook was tried for murder, but was freed under an often used doctrine of "Self-defense." There is no record of what happened to McIvor.

William, or "Billy" (Red Mike) Langan was a typical Virginia City roustabout who seemed to attract trouble without half trying. He was quarrelsome by nature and several times had served time in the local pokey for assault and battery. He was a native of Ireland, somewhat short, at only 5 1/2 feet, about 35 years old with sandy, almost red hair and whiskers framing an "Irish" red face which he accented by usually wearing a reddish brown canvas suit. He was quick of speech and of temper. Mike was somewhat famous locally for his ability to break out of jail. On one occasion he pried out the bricks with a crowbar fashioned from the iron bedstead. But few realized that Red Mike had helped build the court house (and jail) and knew not only the weak points, but that the materials used were worthless. The mortar was like sand; the walls hollow. It took him only 30 minutes to travel through a three foot wall.

~ TWELVE ~

RAILROAD AND SALOONS

The coming of the railroad spawned a string of fronting saloons all across the state. Many early towns were a direct result of the Central Pacific Railroad and, in fact, the railroad often sold the lots that became these towns. All were tough, vibrant and resilient places. Wells, Elko, Palisade, Winnemucca, Lovelock and Reno; all had a "commercial street" on "railroad street," facing the rail line, and on which were lined, side by side, saloons, liquor stores and bawdy houses. Some of these remain today, although most are closed and vacant due to the shifting of traffic to the highways. A prime example is Wells, where these stores are totally deserted. Lovelock is almost similar with only The Ranchhouse and Walk's Place remaining of the 12 or so that once existed. In Reno, the many saloons along Commercial Row, such places as the famous Winehouse, The Owl, Becker's and The Palace, have all been displaced by modern hi-rise casino hotels. Other railroad "towns", such as the Humboldt House and Palisade have totally disappeared. In Winnemucca a few railroad street establishments survive, notably the Martin Hotel. The Winnemucca Hotel, although not fronting the railroad, derived considerable business over the years from the Western Pacific yards and stations directly across the adjoining Humboldt River.

C. P. R. R. Locomotive and Winnemucca Depot - 1868. Photo: Carlos Morales.

The arrival and departure of passenger trains through Elko and other points along the line soon attracted the attention of both the business community and the various town idlers. Those with nothing else to do soon made it a practice to meet every train, to see who was traveling, who was arriving, who was departing, and to exchange small talk in order to collect news of the outside world.

An excerpt from the *Railroad Gazetteer*, the traveler's "Bible" – indicates the Nevada preference for hard cash. This stop was one of the best on the line, featuring shade trees, and fountain and noteworthy meals. It has now vanished.

Humboldt House lies 32 miles northeast of Lovelock at a point where ample water was available. It was founded by the C. P. R. R. in 1868 as an eating station, a place where travelers could disembark and sit at leisure with tablecloths and napkins while the trains were being serviced. It was widely considered an "oasis in the desert" and had the best meals along the line – comparable in every way to the larger Depot Hotel in Reno and the famous Cosmopolitan Hotel in Elko which after 1869 also became The Depot Hotel – featuring 80 rooms, a dining room seating 112, a large bar, billiard room, barber and parlor. Dining cars were added in the 1899 thus eliminating meal stops, however they remained for the stages, and occasionally the trains would stop for mail or sometimes passengers. A post office was in operation there from 1872 to 1919.

Several Nevada towns lived off the railroad in later years, including such places as Carlin, Sparks, Caliente, Winnemucca (which had two lines through town) and Wadsworth.

The Humboldt House with the train in the foreground. This hostelry featured a gushing fountain out front – a rare – and welcome sight for the dusty and tired travelers.

Bakery Saloon – Elko, 1905. Typical turn of the century saloon scene. Photo: Northeastern Nevada Museum. (They must all be teetotalers!)

Another "railroad town" was original Las Vegas. The picture below indicates the Main Street – circa 1927. One bar is offering "fully matured and reimported straight whiskey", whatever that is. This is a rare photo; few exist of Las Vegas before "the Hoover Dam started construction in the early 1930's.

Rawhide, Nevada was a tough camp in a tough environment. It began in 1907 in a particularly arid, desolate area subject to high winds and frequent thunderstorms. Fire was a constant dread and the town suffered many of them. The first occurred on July 20, 1908, a second in September, when almost the entire camp was totally destroyed. Then there were robberies, bank failures and other fires, but the final disaster was a flash flood on August 31, 1909 when a torrent of water down Main and Nevada Streets swept everything into a muddy morass.

The Fountain Saloon on Nevada Street was whirled around by the flood, lifted and carried down the street while all the time the bartender yelled for help and the customers hung on valiantly. Finally the building was settled in a new location, but "was immediately able to dole out the needful" according to the local paper.

But the town was never the same after that. The spirit was still there, but the ore wasn't. Eventually it shrunk to less than 100 souls and then gave up entirely. Some ruins remain but it is difficult to envision what it must have been like.

THIRTEEN

SOME SALOON CATEGORIES

There are essentially three main types of true saloons in Nevada. There are the "Miners" saloons typified usually by those in mining areas, such as Austin, Battle Mountain and Tonopah. Then there are the "Cowboy" saloons, such as still found in Dayton, Elko, Gardnerville and some outlying and isolated locations such as Gerlach and Paradise Valley. And there are the "Farmers" or local saloons, usually more staid operations, such as found in Lovelock, Fallon and Yerington. Occasionally there is a mix of two, or perhaps three types, such as Carvers Station in Smokey Valley and the Taylor Canyon Club north of Elko which gets cowboys from the ranches in the area, miners from the nearby diggings and the locals as well. An exception is when the saloon develops as a service to a special group, such as sportsmen, politicians or hunters for instance – personified by Jarbidge saloons, the Cutthroat in Markleeville and the two bars in Carson City – Jacks and The Globe. No matter what the type these Nevada saloons, especially the older establishments are, they are still focal points of local community interest and affairs and as such serve a definite and positive interest far above just "laying the dust."

Some might be tempted to add a fourth category – the tourist bar. Although all of the current Nevada saloons operate to some extent in this sense, a tourist bar can usually be identified as a function within a gaming casino. There are many examples, almost any casino-hotel qualifies. An exception might be made for the many "old" saloons in Virginia City. While not part of a casino – they are definitely "tourist" in looks and operation. These can hardly be considered old Nevada Saloons – at least in the context of the original "real thing" – and therefore very little attention is paid to them.

It is interesting to note that the decor, patronage and operation of each saloon type often clearly reflected its underlying character and it is therefore relatively easy to determine its type. The subtle gradations which may exist make it all the more interesting.

The map on the following page graphically depicts the generalized location of the various saloons and areas discussed or identified in this analysis.

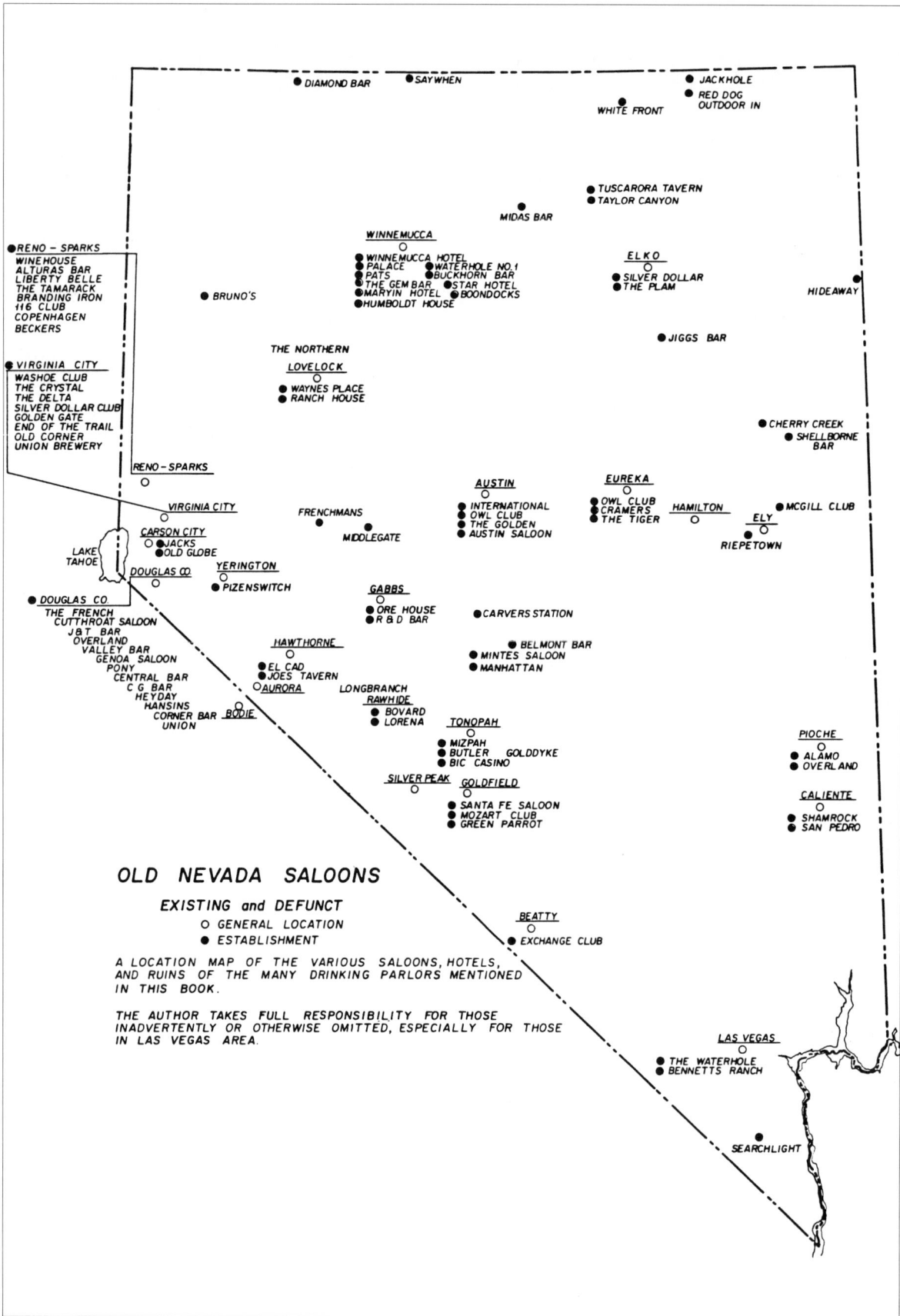

DIAMOND BAR ● ● SAYWHEN ● JACKHOLE
● RED DOG
OUTDOOR IN
WHITE FRONT ●

● TUSCARORA TAVERN
● TAYLOR CANYON
MIDAS BAR ●

WINNEMUCCA ○
WINNEMUCCA HOTEL ●
PALACE ● ● WATERHOLE NO.1
PATS ● ● BUCKHORN BAR
THE GEM BAR ● ● STAR HOTEL
MARYIN HOTEL ● ● BOONDOCKS
HUMBOLDT HOUSE ●

ELKO ○
● SILVER DOLLAR
● THE PLAM

HIDEAWAY ●

BRUNO'S ●

● JIGGS BAR

THE NORTHERN
LOVELOCK ○
● WAYNES PLACE
● RANCH HOUSE

● CHERRY CREEK
● SHELLBORNE
BAR

RENO - SPARKS ○

AUSTIN
● INTERNATIONAL
● OWL CLUB
● THE GOLDEN
● AUSTIN SALOON

EUREKA ○
● OWL CLUB
● CRAMERS
● THE TIGER

HAMILTON
○

● MCGILL CLUB

VIRGINIA CITY ○

FRENCHMANS ●
MIDDLEGATE ●

ELY
○
RIEPETOWN

CARSON CITY ○
○ JACKS
● OLD GLOBE
LAKE
TAHOE
DOUGLAS CO. ○

YERINGTON ○
● PIZENSWITCH

GABBS ○
● ORE HOUSE
● R & D BAR

CARVERS STATION ●

● BELMONT BAR
● MINTES SALOON
● MANHATTAN

HAWTHORNE
○
● EL CAD
● JOES TAVERN
○ AURORA

LONGBRANCH
RAWHIDE
● BOVARD
● LORENA

BODIE ○

TONOPAH ○
● MIZPAH
● BUTLER GOLDDYKE
● BIC CASINO

PIOCHE ○
● ALAMO
● OVERLAND

SILVER PEAK ○
GOLDFIELD ○
● SANTA FE SALOON
● MOZART CLUB
● GREEN PARROT

CALIENTE ○
● SHAMROCK
● SAN PEDRO

OLD NEVADA SALOONS

EXISTING and DEFUNCT
○ GENERAL LOCATION
● ESTABLISHMENT

A LOCATION MAP OF THE VARIOUS SALOONS, HOTELS,
AND RUINS OF THE MANY DRINKING PARLORS MENTIONED
IN THIS BOOK.

THE AUTHOR TAKES FULL RESPONSIBILITY FOR THOSE
INADVERTENTLY OR OTHERWISE OMITTED, ESPECIALLY FOR THOSE
IN LAS VEGAS AREA.

BEATTY ○
● EXCHANGE CLUB

LAS VEGAS ○
● THE WATERHOLE
● BENNETTS RANCH

● SEARCHLIGHT

RENO - SPARKS ○
WINEHOUSE
ALTURAS BAR
LIBERTY BELLE
THE TAMARACK
BRANDING IRON
116 CLUB
COPENHAGEN
BECKERS

VIRGINIA CITY ○
WASHOE CLUB
THE CRYSTAL
THE DELTA
SILVER DOLLAR CLUB
GOLDEN GATE
END OF THE TRAIL
OLD CORNER
UNION BREWERY

DOUGLAS CO. ●
THE FRENCH
CUTTHROAT SALOON
J & T BAR
OVERLAND
VALLEY BAR
GENOA SALOON
PONY
CENTRAL BAR
C G BAR
HEYDAY
HANSINS
CORNER BAR
UNION

FOURTEEN

SALOONS OF CARSON CITY

There were three "community focus" most popular saloons in early Carson City; surprisingly two of them are still active.

The long defunct and probably most popular and influential saloon was the famous Ormsby House. This three story edifice encompassing 100 rooms stood on the northwest corner of Carson (Main Street) and 2nd Street and was commenced in 1860 by Major William Ormsby, who soon sold it to the George Gibson Company. He was killed later that year in the Pyramid Lake War with the Paiutes. It was one of the earliest hotels and from the beginning the acknowledged site of unofficial political activity as well as the social cynosure of the incipient community. Late in 1872, a wooden addition was built on the corner lot which was cleverly joined to the original brick structure. During the following years a number of different owners managed the operation; in 1885 for instance it was under the control of a party named Kaiser who offered a European plan, a novelty in this area. The hotel was closed in 1894 and stood vacant until 1931 when it was sold to Dominic Laxalt, proprietor of the French Hotel on North Carson street. It was subsequently torn down.

In 1971, Paul Laxalt, son of Dominic (and later Governor of the state & senator) began construction of a new "Ormsby House" at a different location, selling it in 1975. It is still in operation, has been expanded and remodeled and is still (somewhat) the center of current political intrigue and machinations. But it is really now a Casino-Hotel—not the same thing at all.

Jack's Bar:

Located on the corner of 5th and Main Streets in central Carson City (across from the present Ormsby House), is the oldest continuing business at the same location in the city. This site has been in constant use since it began as a dance hall in 1859. In 1899 a totally new building was erected, called the Bank Saloon. In 1920, an antique and ornate twenty foot mahogany back bar, said to have been carved in Bavaria, was acquired from the Ormsby County Courthouse's Magnolia Saloon.[1] During prohibition Pete Pierini and Virgil Bucchieneri (who also owned the Globe) renamed it as the Bank Resort (saloons then being out of favor), which sold demure soda water up front but rot gut whiskey (from a secret still in Lyon County) out back. Since this building backed to the red-light district a lot of business took place through the back door. During subsequent years the operation was named: Hernando's Hideaway (in 1956), the Y-NOT Bar (in 1960), and then Angelo's. In 1966 Jack Fowler and Joe Brown bought it and it then became Jack's Bar, as it remains today. Its thirty-two foot bar is in usual heavy use, mainly serving locals, and is especially so during the biennial legislative sessions since the Legislative Chambers are directly across Main Street (U. S. 395). It is cluttered but still exudes a certain charm and patina only time can provide. While it does not have the traditional "naked lady" in a gilt frame over the back bar there are, as can plainly be seen, several somewhat lascivious pictures which connote the same thing. It is definitely one of the last character saloons left in the state.

---

1) The only bar in Nevada which ever operated inside a courthouse.

Exterior of <u>Jack's Bar</u> in Carson City. Photo: By author.

<u>Jack's Bar</u>, interior 1991. It really hasn't changed much in 50 years. Photo: By the author.

The other main emporium the Old Globe Saloon, a very old establishment dating back to the very origins of Carson City, it was originally located on Main Street between Telegraph and Spear Streets in the very heart of the original community. The building, only some 25 feet wide, was built in 1874 and featured a boarding house upstairs. In 1881 it opened as the "Globe Saloon and Club Rooms." It was first operated by Andrew Robert who continued operations until 1954 when Bucchianeri and Pierini purchased it. In 1970 the saloon was moved to Curry Street directly behind the original location. It featured then (and now) a long polished bar along one side and a room full of memorabilia including many early photos of the V & T Railroad and Comstock workings, as well as group pictures of various athletic teams, with some yellowed newspaper clippings and a great picture of an old bar the night before prohibition. Bartenders in the early days, when they served a customer, often put a Remington cap and ball .45 on the bar first, then the glass, then the bottle, a vivid discouragement to any patron tempted to pour too large a glassful. This all happened many years ago when it was the Nevada custom to put the bottle and the glass on the bar and let the drinker pour his own. This is only done now in the movies (John Wayne was pictured many times practicing this method) and, until recently, at the Old Globe Saloon in Carson City. The sign remains, however, framed and hung behind the new bar – "gentlemen may pour their own; ladies need not, and hogs will not."

Interior of the Globe Saloon, 1991. Photo: By the author.

THE "WHEEL BARROW" MAN

One summer evening in 1878 six longtime citizens of Elko were having a "drop" or two in the Elko Saloon (their favorite) while discussing the events of the day. Elko was ten years old by then, a thriving and growing community.

They were all good friends even though they worked in various trades and they often met for a social hour before dinner. Harvey Adams, the local constable, an affable man, was sort of the "leader" of the group, although Monk Peters and Jim Ashwood were usual partakers. The talk rambled as usual, turning to beards for a while (all but Adams wore heavy whiskers), then to a current national news item reporting the western movement of the "wheelbarrow man". It seems that an R. L. Potter was pushing a wheelbarrow from New York City to San Francisco as a result of a barroom bet and was last reported passing through Wells, only a few miles east of Elko. His entrance into Elko could not be far away.

The following evening the town was electrified when the news flashed from saloon to saloon that the "wheelbarrow man" was coming. The entire town it seemed turned out for the affair and soon, sure enough, from the east, trudging along the railroad tracks, appeared a man pushing a fully loaded wheelbarrow. He seemed capable of this task although his long hair and beard gave him a distinctly unkempt appearance.

But he didn't stop, just kept going on through town. This was too much for the "boys" and several of them, including Peters and Ashwood, finally persuaded him to tarry a while for a few glasses of beer.

He reluctantly agreed and everyone adjourned to the Elko Saloon where this Mr. Potter amazed all by his prodigious ability to consume as many beers as were placed before him.

This went on for some time. The wheelbarrow man quaffing, laughing and quaffing again and again. Eventually it was Monk Peters who figured it out. The wheelbarrow man wasn't Mr. Potter at all—it was their old friend Harvey Adams (with a fake beard) who had just pulled the prank of the year on his friends and the town. Upon this discovery, with much laughter and backslapping, he had to buy the drinks for the rest of the evening which he did with great good humor.

A day later the real Mr. Potter wheeled into town. His wheelbarrow was loaded with 70 pounds and he said he was 134 days out of New York City. He was 45 years old and had dark hair and whiskers, both enormously long. He was treated royally and soon departed westerly replenished with ample food and booze. Later it was determined that there was no wager and no trip. Mr. Potter was also freeloading, but with a most ingenious scheme-but Harvey Adams had gotten the best of him-at least in Elko.

FIFTEEN

OLD SALOONS OF AUSTIN

One of the early Nevada boom towns which freely recognized the local saloons as the main, if not only, centers of attraction and conviviality, was the mid-state and very remote community of Austin, in southern Lander County. Located in a moderately steep canyon on the western flank of the Toiyabe "backbone" range, this settlement began in 1862, peaked in 1865, and has been declining, slowly, ever since.

The *Reese River Reveille*, Austin's famous newspaper and only serious in-state rival to Virginia City's *Enterprise* reported, on 19 April, 1884:

> "New saloon-John L. Hale, late of Clifton, has fitted up and opened one of the neatest saloons in Austin, near the corner of Main and Virginia Streets. The floor is finely carpeted, the bar handsomely fitted up and well furnished, comfortable easy chairs, tables, newspapers and superb lunch with polite and handsome bartenders are among the attraction of the Merchants Exchange. We prophesy that Hale will get what he deserves to have, a good share of the public patronage, and that his Merchants Exchange will be no misnomer, but a fair exchange of good money for good drink."

An advertisement in that same paper reported;

"Mammoth Lager Beer Saloon, in the basement, corner of Main and Virginia Streets, Austin, Nevada (same corner?). Choice liquors, wines, lager beer and cigars served by pretty girls who understand their business and attend to it. Votaries of Bacchus Gambrinus, Venus or Cupid can spend an evening agreeable at the Mammoth Saloon." (It actually wasn't anything like this.)

Main Street (U. S. 50) through Austin 1992. It didn't look a loot different in 1892. Photo: By the author.

Early Austin saloon, 1915. Photo: Nevada Historical Society, Reno.

The picture above and the one on the facing page are classics. These early day photographs depict Austin saloons of a slightly later date, about 1915. Note the differences between the two. One has an air of gentility; quite obviously a "classier" establishment; the other is much plainer with only painted panels, several rather nondescript framed pictures and a more "barren" look. In both these "frozen moments" everyone is drinking what appears to be straight shots, except the mustached man in the vest, who has one in each hand.

There is no "Naked Lady" painting; but two fully dressed and demure ladies – advertising some brand of beer, will have to do.

A little known, but highly appropriate early day activity in Austin was the Sazerac Lying Club, named for a then favorite brand of brandy. It was headquartered in one of the many saloons of the town (which no longer exists). The members, all respected citizens of the community, would convene "before the plank" in this bar after work to draw a few and to tell the biggest lies possible. There was always copious liquefied refreshment (and sometimes money) at stake to keep all of them totally involved. The club lasted many years and eventually attracted a national audience.

Austin saloon circa 1912. Photo: Nevada Historical Society, Reno.

There were until recently still four old bars operating in the town even though the population has now dwindled to only about 300. All still reflect the hardier days of long ago. Two appear rather dismal from the outside; The Austin Saloon (formerly Vance and Arlene's) and the Owl Club (which features a green Irish elf painted on the facade, plus a garish rainbow) and which was formerly a theater. The Golden, a simple structure, has been in business since the 1930's (formerly a buggy shop during prohibition) and which possesses a truly magnificent cherry wood Brunswick bar and back bar, complete with the original mirrors, with no slots and no pool table, but there are deer heads, old signs, and other back country mementoes. This bar hasn't materially changed in fifty years – but it is now closed following the death of Clara – the long time character owner, barkeep and croupier (at the blackjack table).

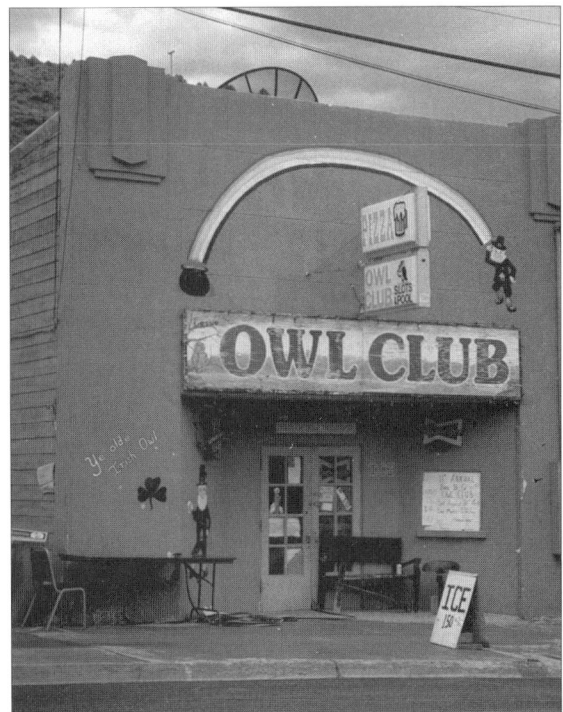

Owl Club–Modern Austin. Photo: by the author.

The main remaining older still operating saloon in Austin is the historic and venerable International Hotel at Cedar and Main Streets (U. S. 50). This ancient two story wooden building was built in Virginia City in 1860, then dismantled and moved in its entirety to Austin in 1863, in order to make room for a larger and more pretentious structure. Austin is 180 miles from the Comstock and roads (if they could be called that at that time) were minimal. However, lumber was exceedingly dear in central Nevada since all building materials (and everything else) was freighted from western Nevada or more frequently California. Much of the hotel burned in 1958. However, the original bar and restaurant survived. The back bar was built in England in about 1850, shipped around the horn to San Francisco and then freighted to Virginia City. It is, as are all Brunswick products, a master piece of cabinetry and the half inch thick plate crystal mirror is the original.

Back bar at the International. Photo: By the author, 1992.

Early Austin's wide-open gambling resorts were, like its brothels, seldom mentioned in the chaste columns of the *Reveille*, yet they were long a conspicuous feature of the life of the town. A. D. Richardson, a correspondent for the *New York Tribune*, thus described them (in 1865): "At night the brilliantly lighted gambling saloons, with open fronts, are filled with a motley crowd. Women conduct the games at several monte tables, shuffling the cards and handling the piles of silver coins with the unruffled serenity of professional gamblers; while men of all classes "fight the tiger" with the usual earnestness of that fascinating pursuit."

SIXTEEN

OLD SALOONS OF DAYTON

<u>End</u> <u>of</u> <u>the</u> <u>Trail</u>: An old building, dating from about 1900, this wooden structure in the heart of Dayton (Lyon County) features a large open saloon in front and a restaurant in the rear, serving steaks, chicken, some Mexican dishes and sweet breads! The saloon itself has high ceilings, an abundance of "Junk" items, both on the walls and the ceiling to peruse, including a lot of fight memoranda. It has a definite aura of being a "Cowboy" bar (which it is). It's clientele obviously is still "real" cowboy, "fake" cowboy, some locals (men and women) and an occasional hippie type left over from ten years or so ago. There are also now many construction workers, surveyors and the like, reflecting the building activity now overtaking the Dayton area. A fun place, especially in the evenings, when almost anything (always unsuspected) can and does happen. The food is good as well; how often do we find sweetbreads–in a cowboy bar in rural Nevada?

<u>End of the Trail Saloon</u>, Dayton Nevada, 1991. Photo: By the author.

The <u>Old Corner Bar</u> is located on the corner of Main and Pike Streets in Dayton. This ancient one room saloon's main claim to fame is that it served as a set for the "Misfits," a 1961 film starring Marilyn Monroe and Clark Gable. The building was originally established after the 1870 fire, serving as a general store and a garage before World War II. It now has an old bar across one end, numerous old posters and pictures and lots of slot machines. Food is served in the back. See pictures on the following page.

Old Corner Bar – Photo: The author, 1991.

This old picture is of an earlier Dayton era when the Dayton Club, now demolished, and the adjoining bar, which featured Sierra Beer on tap (a brand now out of production) was the center of town. This adjoining bar, with some changes, is now the End of the Trail. Photo: Nevada Department of Economic Development.

SEVENTEEN

AN OLD SALOON IN GOLDFIELD

The Santa Fe Saloon – in Goldfield! This out-of-the-way place (at least five blocks from the main highway U. S. 395) is in an otherwise almost totally deserted "ghost town," even though it is the County Seat. This unique building was originally constructed in 1905 at the peak of the Goldfield Boom and therefore lays claim to be the oldest "continually operating" saloon in the state.[1] While operating strictly as a local bar, it has recently become a major attraction and pit-stop for many of the more knowledgeable travelers between Reno and Las Vegas. But only for those who know it's there; it surely isn't a stop-by tourist place at all.

Its remote location on the edge of town enabled its historic claim to longevity; for it allowed it to survive the 1913 flood and the 1923 fire, both of which devastated the community. The bar room is original, but with some additions over the years; the original Brunswick back bar, always an important and imposing element, remains. The rest of the interior is also unusual – a museum of mining and other memorabilia including hoisting bells, a life-size dummy of Wyatt Earp (supposedly), and some framed historic newspapers. There are also a few slots, a card table, and lots of caps tacked to the ceiling. Many of these reflect the names of motorcycle clubs and garages from all over California.

Santa Fe Saloon – Goldfield. Photo: Scott Smith.

---

1) Which may-or may not, be true. The "continuous" aspect is the key. Genoa Bar – in Genoa, is the oldest – but not the oldest continually operating establishment – is the claim.

For many years the place was owned by Jim Grogan a hirsute, potbellied eccentric, one of the last of a vanishing breed of character saloon keepers. The present owner is Jim Marsh, an auto dealer from Las Vegas, who is ably assisted by "Pat" – the lady barkeep. She has been there since 1986, replacing Rosemary Cali who was also a legend in her own right. The place has low ceilings, an uneven board floor and appears rather ramshackle – but it is certainly quaint. It must rank high on anyone's list of Nevada's little known treasures.

Interior of <u>Santa Fe Saloon</u>. Photo: By Scott Smith.

There are several other older saloons in Goldfield, notwithstanding its minuscule population. These include the <u>Mozart Club</u>, which also features a restaurant and a 1905 back bar and the <u>Green Parrot Saloon</u>, offering "The Penny Bar", a character place which is not always open.

⊰ ⊱

BEER $1.00
SOFT DRINKS $1.00
WHISKEY $1.50
FANCY SHIT $3.50
Sign – in a Nevada bar

EIGHTEEN

OLD SALOONS OF WINNEMUCCA

Winnemucca, located at an easy crossing of the Humboldt River, began early, and rapidly developed as a transportation hub for a vast section of central Nevada. This was accelerated after 1868, when the Central Pacific Railroad (now the Southern Pacific) came through town, and more so when the Western Pacific arrived in 1908. These two railroad trains are some five blocks apart, one on each end of Bridge Street, the main connecting commercial thoroughfare. This street soon became the main commercial center of retail establishments and other uses, including all the bars in town, which were lined along this route. This resulted in a lively and often congested mud roadway crowded with people, wagons and livestock.

Between 1868 and 1874 Winnemucca grew to 1,600 people and by 1890 it boasted 15 stores, three hotels, 21 saloons, three livery stables, five blacksmiths, a hospital, telegraph office, post office, express office and an assay office as well as two schools, two churches (and two clergymen), two lawyers, six doctors and 12 "others."

Of these early day saloons, a few became more popular, serving the community as gathering places and centers where "tanglefoot" could readily be imbibed. These included such original locations as Oasis Bar on the corner of Bridge and 2nd Streets, Telegraph Saloon, near the Farris Hotel, Scotty's Club, The Capitol Saloon, The Palace and The Bud, Depot Bar at Lay and the S. P. R. R. tracks, Becker's Saloon on Bridge at the railroad track (in the basement) and the Star Hotel, which was later demolished for reconstruction as the Star Broiler. Busch Hotel was a popular spot too, until it burned in 1924, after escaping a similar threat in October, 1900).[1] The Busch was a railroad facility – facing the Central Pacific tracks.

There were still 17 bars in Winnemucca in 1925; they lined Bridge Street from one railroad line to the other. But as the 1930's came, so did changes to the saloon scene. New establishments began operations, including the Miners Bar (later replaced by the Farris Hotel) which in its day was a wild spot, especially on pay day at the mines; the Mint Club on the corner of Bridge and 3rd Streets (now Ben's Liquors) which featured a French girl singer - quite glamorous for this Nevada cow town; The Frontier, next to the Bakery and the Buckhorn Bar, near the Gem.

Today it is hard to identify a true saloon in the manner of the old tradition. The closest one to it is perhaps Boon Docks, on Bridge Street between 2nd and 3rd Streets. This old bar has a great cherry back bar, only a few slots and the distinctive "atmosphere" so necessary, but difficult to create.

---

1) Fire was a constant threat in these early, mostly wooden towns. An August 1905 fire swept away most structures on both sides of the block on Bridge Street between 2nd and 3rd Streets.

Cherry back bar at the <u>Boon Docks</u> in Winnemucca. Photo: By the author.

<u>Boon</u> <u>Docks</u> is currently the favorite haunt of various civic leaders who usually adjourn to this location after late night sessions. The open meeting law has severely constricted the previous free wheeling conversations, arguments, and sometimes, decisions.

<u>Winnemucca</u> <u>Hotel</u>. The building was constructed in 1863 by Lay and Company, but did not formally open until December 1866. Lay originally came from France to build the Humboldt Canal. In 1867, Frank Baud, a well known local entrepreneur, bought it, but he died a year later and the Lay brothers regained control. In October, 1871, D. Giroux erected a large two story wooden building adjacent to the earlier adobe structure which was completed in time for a fabulous 4th of July day "Grand Ball." It has since operated continuously under many managements. A flood in 1910, was "threatening" and an earthquake in 1915 sheared off a chimney, otherwise the building today is much the same as then. The massive oak bar, still a prominent feature, came around the horn and was laboriously transshipped to this desert midpoint by railroad.

The establishment always enjoyed a loyal clientele from the personnel of the Western Pacific (railroad) who's yards were just across the river, but now it is a major tourist attraction as well serving family meals to residents, ranchers and miners, who happen to be in town. The place still has the old time ambience which is so appealing.

Bar in the <u>Winnemucca Hotel</u> – 1990. Photo: By the author.

At the other end of town, opposite the freight depot of the Southern Pacific tracks was the opposite anchor the <u>Busch</u> <u>Hotel</u>, on Railroad Street. This was a two story wood frame structure typical of the times. It was completed in 1888 and contained a parlor, 14 bedrooms, a fine dining room and a bar together with a card room and the usual service elements. The usual arcade stretched across the front. The building was sixty feet long by thirty feet wide with a forty by fifteen foot addition. The hotel burned completely on December 24, 1924 (Christmas Eve, which must have been a real catastrophe), but while it lasted it was a popular local eating and watering spot.

<u>Busch Hotel</u> – a street scene about 1900.
Obviously a summer affair – possibly the Fourth of July? Photo: Humboldt County Museum.

In between were two other notable libation parlors. These were <u>The Palace Saloon</u> and the <u>Gem</u>. Both are gone now, but are remembered as active and popular places. An early day picture of <u>The Palace</u> is shown below. Note the covered arcade quite common in early Nevada. <u>The Palace</u> was one of the earliest real saloons in the town; this building was in existence prior to 1884. It was located on Bridge Street, between 3rd and 4th Streets. It is now the J. C. Penney's Store.

Twelve horse freight team in front of <u>The Palace</u> <u>Saloon</u> in Winnemucca. Photo: Courtesy of Carlos Morales.

A later day picture of <u>The Palace</u>, 1905, still indicates the wooden sidewalk, the swinging doors and the hitching rail, but the arcade is gone. Chub Moore, Sr. (center) was the bartender and sheriff.
Photo: Nevada Historical Society.

The one bar that is most fondly remembered in Winnemucca is the <u>Gem</u>, located on the corner of Bridge and 2nd Streets. This establishment was first named the <u>Railroad</u> <u>Saloon</u> when it opened in March 10, 1869. It was a large frame structure fitted up in the "most elegant style." Later it was successively called the <u>Old</u> <u>Corner</u> <u>Saloon</u> and <u>Timmons</u> <u>Saloon</u>. In August 1905, a fire engulfed the entire block; the original wooden building disappeared forever to be replaced by a new red brick building which opened in 1909, again as a saloon, "like a Phoenix rising from the ashes." The following years saw still more name changes – it was the <u>Central</u> in 1922. But for over 50 years it was known universally as the "cowboy" bar – especially for the Paradise Valley buckaroos.

During the period of the '50's, '60's, and '70's this bar was a very popular local gathering place, especially for political and social groups in the town. Many important civic decisions were hammered out in the somewhat Spartan surroundings. The old <u>Gem</u> came to an ignominious and unpopular end in about 1982, when it was wrecked as part of the rebuilding program of the Star Hotel and Casino, (mostly Casino). Many of the town's leading citizens stood by and wept as the wrecker's ball demolished this piece of local history and many stated that the new Star would never be successful because of it. And it never was.

A very rare photograph of the interior of the <u>Gem</u>, taken in 1943, courtesy of Irene Scott, Winnemucca

August 1981 – Beginning the demolition of the <u>Gem</u> about 1982. Photo: Irene Scott.

The <u>Star</u> <u>Hotel</u> (really a rooming house) began operations about 1900, at the corner of Bridge and 3rd Streets. This two story wooden hotel catered to the sheepherders during the winter months. It operated this way for some years (although called the <u>El Dorado</u> for awhile) the building was destroyed by fire in 1905 and rebuilt, first as the "<u>New</u> <u>Reception</u>," but by 1915 reverting to the <u>Star</u> <u>Cafe</u> or just <u>The Star</u>. After 1930 it became a gambling hall and in 1957, Joe Mackie secured a lease eventually opening it as the <u>New</u> <u>Star</u> <u>Broiler</u> <u>and</u> <u>Casino</u> in March, 1958. In 1978 it too burned. The site was vacant until April, 1981 when the new owners acquired the remainder of the half block, including the Farris Hotel (erected in 1938), the <u>Gem Bar</u>, the Eagle Drug Store and Robinson's Barber Shop, all of which were demolished in order to build the <u>New</u> <u>Star</u>. This operation is now closed and inoperative.

The Buckhorn: A great saloon while it lasted, unfortunately it did not last long. The picture below includes several prominent and remembered citizens and a Mexican Vaquero.

Interior of the <u>Buckhorn Bar</u> – 1904. Photo: Courtesy Nevada Historical Society.

Pat's Bar

This establishment, only 25 feet wide, is also on Bridge Street and is over 100 years old. The place was run by "Pat" a genial Irishman for 40 years, and now by "Pat" (really Patricia) for the last 16 years. A pure drinking bar, catering to an established local clientele, it can sometimes be a fun place, especially on a snowy night.

Winnemucca also offers a distinctive uniqueness in the still legal operation of five in-town brothels, including "My Place" and the "Cozy Corner," both in the Bell Addition at the end of Baud Street (named for Frank Baud, an early area pioneer and not what you might think). Only the <u>Cozy Corner</u> is advertised as a "Bar", however. Drinks run mostly to short beers and are indeed secondary to the main purposes and attractions of the house. They are "different" and are almost all that is left of a once flourishing industry that was very active in many of the smaller and remote early Nevada towns.

An unidentified saloon in early Reno. Both the front and back bar are especially notable, note the brass foot bar and the ubiquitous spittoons. What is the bartender's headgear?

⚜ ⚜

"...were the drinking saloons; some with costly pictures, mirrors and decanters, others with plain counters and black bottles, but all dispensing the staple Washoe beverage of whiskey to their insatiable patrons. At all hours of the day, but in the evening particularly, the movement in and out of these saloons and along the principal streets was like the flow of a twisting stream over a rocky bed, apparently seeking an outlet at every point, but turning back with swollen waters towards the stream again and again. Or, in some odd way, as one watches the flow, it brought to mind the circling tramp of a tiger, snuffling at bar after bar of his cage. Perhaps this was because the city, set in the desert, had something prison-like in its encircling walls of barren hills and few thought of straying beyond its circle of lights."

Elliot Lord – Comstock Miners & Mining.

NINETEEN

OLD SALOONS IN RENO-SPARKS

In the early days of Reno, most of the saloons were lined up on Commercial Row - facing the railroad tracks which was then the main focus and reason for being. Most of these establishments were long and narrow with high ceilings, a long polished bar on one side, a few tables on the other. Bar lunches were prevalent and the general atmosphere most pleasant but somewhat dark and possibly even dingy. Many older Renoites have fond memories of the Wine House, Becker's, the Palace and the Nevada Club.

In 1915 Reno boasted 34 Hotels (many of which were really rooming houses) and 67 saloons, including such old stalwarts as the "116" Club, The Palace, The Riverside Hotel and the old Waldorf. As downtown Reno grew into its current "metropolitan" status, these properties were bought and amalgamated into larger holdings for reconstruction as large resort hotel Casino's such as we know them today. As a result the few remaining examples of older area bars mainly exist on East 4th Street towards Sparks, such as the Spot, the Alturas and Coney Island. These all have an origin date of about 1945 and all were related to then U. S. 40 which was Fourth Street.

In that year, Reno, which then boasted a population of about 31,000, supported 85 "lounges, beer parlors and nightclubs." Many of these were still on Commercial Row, including the Winehouse, Oberon, Martins Bar, the Owl Club and Becker's[1], in some cases side by side. Virginia Street had eleven such places in town, plus three more farther out[2] (Mt. Rose Street was the end of town at the time) while Sierra Street hosted six and Center Street had seven. Second Street was busy dispensing drinks too, with 11 such establishments and 4th Street (the main highway) had six, somewhat more spread out. Sparks, at a population then of about 3,000, had eleven pubs, all on 4th Street (with the single exception of the Copenhagen Bar on Prater Way (which is still there but at a different location). During the last 45 years, most of them have disappeared (and of course a lot of new ones have appeared), but a few, a very few, are still operating at their original locations.

---

1) Roos and Becker Brewery was originally established in Washoe City, in 1866. It was then known to "be so cool and inviting that a man cannot be more or less human to pass it by." They served free dark rye bread, cold meats, sausages, Swiss and Limburger cheese with mustard and pickles. In July 1867 Beckers bought out Roos, and in January 1868 the saloon burned to the ground. Beckers then moved to Reno where he opened the well known Beckers on Commercial Row.

2) Notably the Tamarack, which is still there and still operating as it always has.

One of the better and most popular of these bars was the Wine House, a narrow long(25') and dark saloon with a bar on one side, a back bar filled with bottles – all neatly arranged and wine barrels on the other side. The pictures below are very rare.

Interior: Wine House. Photo: Courtesy the Frankovich Family, Reno.

Interior: Wine House. Photo: Courtesy the Frankovich Family, Reno.

Exterior view of commercial row in Reno 1911 showing the "Line" of bars, liquor emporiums and dance halls. Mr. M. Leter's Clothing Store seems strangely out of place. Photo: Courtesy Marshall Fey, Reno.

Gambling in early Reno took place mainly in the back alleys, especially Douglas Alley, where The Bank Club, Rex Club and the Winehouse provided games. The atmosphere was generally dark and dingy, quiet and very unglamorous, not at all like the garish, well-lighted environs of the present day casinos. The picture below, taken in about 1910, indicates this.

Photo: Courtesy Marshall Fey.

Some of Reno and Sparks "Older" establishments which are still in operation are:

The Baron: (4th Street at 6th) originally the Eastside Inn, it was one of several bars scattered along East 4th Street catering to the traffic flows when it was then Highway 40. In those days there was little nearby housing, the area between Reno and Sparks were vacant fields. Over the years it has seen numerous remodeling; it now espouses a veritable forest of pecky cedar with a sort of 1930 decor. And is now more of a lounge with a fireplace, pool tables and live music.

Spot Bar: B Street at Sullivan Lane is also one of the older local relics, dating (at least) from 1946. It has a pool table, some slots and a local clientele, but essentially it is "just a bar."

Copenhagen: On Prater Way near Sullivan Lane is really the "new Copenhagen" having only been there some 26 years. The original bar was adjacent to the Coney Island, but was moved (in order to build the freeway), then moved again to the present location.

116 Club: (Now called the Stein of the Times) at 116 No. Center Street is the only original remaining in-town old bar. It has, over many years, been known by a number of names including the Alpine, Winery (in 1915) and the Alta, but since 1946, it has been the 116 Club, featuring a long and distinguished bar and back bar, good food and ten different tap beers.

Alturas Bar: (Now Alturas Lounge) although in existence for at least 50 years (but not continuously at this location, having started on East 2nd Street), this is still a popular drinking hangout. There are some slots in back, a pool table, and (surprisingly) lots of light since two sides of this corner bar feature large glass expanses to the adjoining streets.[2] There is no particular antique flavor. However, it is primarily a gathering place for a steady clientele who all seem to know each other.

Coney Island Bar: In existence since 1946 (it was a tamale factory prior to that) Galetti's place has earned a deserved reputation for good food and conviviality over the years. The bar itself is lackluster. There is no back bar at all, but the large barny room is usually full and noisy, especially on Friday evenings when the college kids fill the place.

Liberty Belle Saloon and Restaurant: At 4250 So. Virginia Street, near the Convention Center looks like an "old bar" but really isn't, having been erected in the early 1960's. The interior is pleasantly "cluttered" with old things, including some distinguished old chandeliers and hand lettered sign, and a sort of museum of early slot machines.[3] A main attraction is the magnificent back bar which originally graced the old "Owl Bar and Cafe." This turn of the century libation parlor was first at 232 North Virginia Street between where Harold's Club and The Nevada Club now stand before it was moved, in 1920, to Commercial Row. Twelve years later it was renamed the Pasttime. In 1955 it was again moved to the corner of Douglas Alley and Sierra Street until that building was razed, in 1960 for the construction of the Primadonna. The bar was bought in 1961 (for $250) and installed in the Liberty Belle in 1963 which required the ceiling to be raised to fit it. This is perhaps the best of the old time bars (at least in feeling) left in Reno. The attached restaurant serves copious and inexpensive food in a somewhat busy and noisy atmosphere.

---

2)   This is unusual since most saloons affect a certain gloom atmosphere.

3)   The Feys, owners and operators were the inventors of the modern slot machine.

4)   The old Owl had lots of company; it was near the Carroll (214 No. Virginia), the Budweiser (244 No. Virginia) and across the street from the Monarch Saloon (225 No. Virginia) and The Snug (231 No. Virginia) in 1915.

Photo: Courtesy Marshall Fey

The Tamarack, on South Virginia Street (in Reno) has been there since 1946 making it one of the oldest saloons in the area. This log cabin bar is usually a boisterous place; minor fights, arm-wrestling, dancing, pool playing are the usual pastimes, but drinking is the mainstay. Everyone seems to have a perpetual good time-which is the essence of any bar.

There are three other (now closed) Reno saloons that deserve recognition. First (and best) of these was the justly famous Corner Bar[5] in the old Riverside Hotel. Long a top gathering place for the movers and shakers of the Reno scene, this venerable bar with its tall frosted glass doors opening to the intersection of Island Avenue and South Virginia Street was truly a "great place." The others are the old Waldorf, a most popular hangout, particularly with the college set, and the Townhouse, on West First Street. This was also a fine restaurant until it burned down in the mid '50's, to be reopened as Vario's on South Virginia Street.

---

4)   The only real competition to the Corner Bar was the long bar in the old Golden Hotel on Center Street.

Saloons located where they could; sometimes up-stairs, such as the Washoe Club in Virginia City (a very restricted millionaire's hangout reachable by a circular staircase) and sometimes in basements, such as shown above as the Pyramid House, operating in the new City of Reno in the 1870's. This structure was on the southwest corner of Commercial Row and Lake Street and later became the China Club. It's a vacant parking lot today. Nevada Historical Society photo.

Although not actually in Reno or Sparks, one of the oldest saloons in Washoe County is the Washoe Bar[6] in what is left of Washoe City – in Washoe Valley, some 20 miles south of Reno.

In 1867 Washoe City boasted ten saloons, all of which catered to all "except Indians, Chinese and women." These included: Will Williams, J. D. Roberts, Pete Brows, the French Saloon, the Bank Exchange, the Sazarac, and Sam Southworths. The Magnolia Saloon, formerly the Oriental, had a "room quite large, warm and pleasant, well furnished with easy chairs and side chairs where leisure hours can be passed pleasantly." There were also the Teamsters Resort, the Fashion Saloon and the Washoe City Saloon (instituted in January 1863).

Washoe City boomed until 1885 – mostly based on teaming and freight activities to Virginia City, but began to decline in 1870-71 when it lost the county seat to Reno. By 1880 it was a "dilapidated hamlet" with a population of only about 200. (In 1894 the post office closed, the usual death knell) "only one of the commercial structures was left" (Paher, page 43). That was, and is, the Washoe Bar. During prohibition it operated as a grocery store but reverted to a bar as soon as it was legal to do so. The newer portion in the rear was added in 1972. It is a low-ceilinged, rustic sort of place with an affable barkeep (Sandy).

---

6)   Also knows as the Sh-Boom Saloon – don't ask why.

TWENTY

OLD SALOONS OF VIRGINIA CITY

Virginia City represented, indisputably, the acme of social (and other) drinking in the halcyon days of Nevada mining. From its inception until about 1900, saloons were prolific, numbering in the hundreds, and "baiting the tiger" was a respectable and desirous thing to do—at all hours it seems.

By 1890, following the disastrous fire of 1875, the number of saloons serving the city had diminished somewhat from the earlier peak years, but even then there were some 30 bars, only a few of which are still recognizable as familiar names today. Some of these outstanding places of those days which have survived (more or less) are: The Sazerac, (see picture below) which actually began in 1859, but more recently has degraded to an ice-cream parlor.[1]

The old Sazerac Saloon, Virginia City. Photo: Nevada Historical Society.

---

1)   Although it appears to be closed and inoperative now. Other recognizable holdovers are The Delta, The Union Brewery, The Washoe Club, the Bucket of Blood (not it's original name) and of course, The Crystal Bar.

Not all of these early day saloons displayed the class of the Sazerac. Many, if not most, were dark, drab affairs, with a mahogany bar along one side and nothing (or possibly a few tables) along the other. A case in point is the picture below—of an unknown Virginia City saloon of the 1890's.

Virginia City Saloon. Photo: Nevada Historical Society.

One can't help but wonder as to the demise of the others - some with such tantalizing names as: Old Magnolia, (16 South "C" Street) "Mike Feeney's or the "William Tell" (45 South "C" Street). During the quiet years, from about 1900 to 1945, the number of operating establishments varied, declining to ten or so during prohibition and the depression. However, through the years The Delta (saloon and restaurant), The Crystal Bar, and several others survived.

There are at the moment still some 18 operating saloons now officially called (rather tamely) "cocktail lounges," or sometimes "taverns," operating in Virginia City. The number and names change almost weekly. These range from the older established institutions such as The Crystal Bar, The Delta, the Bucket of Blood and the Brass Rail to the newer, smaller (and more ephemeral) outlets such as "Cowboys and Indians," Calamity Jane's (whose namesake had absolutely nothing to do with Virginia City) and the Mark Twain Saloon. Most are still great fun and most are a welcome relief to the plethora of candy stores, T-shirt printers and "Old time" photographers, which otherwise clutter up and cheapen the real Virginia City experience.[2]

---

2) Some of the smaller places have now found it economically necessary to combine the bar operation with candy, T-shirts, photos, food and whatever as a sort of encompassing "tourist trap." It isn't real, it isn't pretty, but it pays the bills. In some cases it is even hard to find the bar.

The 18 still operating saloons seem to divide naturally into three basic groups: These are those who call themselves "bars" or "saloons" but in reality are not that at all. These places are primarily fast food purveyors; such places as the Mark Twain Saloon, Palace (Saloon and Restaurant), Solid Muldoon's, Brass Rail (features "home cooking"), and Calamity Jane's" (which is often jammed with children). The Silver Stope serves food as an evening restaurant, but also has a small bar and jazz every Sunday night. Secondly, there are the straight out tourist places which have a little of everything, including a bar (of sorts), food (of sorts), but also T-shirts, gifts, "old time" photos, baseball caps, and of course the ubiquitous slot machine. The places include: the Ponderosa Saloon, the Red Garter (with very nice leaded glass front doors), Bonanza Saloon (Land and Cattle Company) which has a good view down Six Mile Canyon, lots of slots and a pervading smell of popcorn, the Bucket of Blood, has no back bar but some lovely old hanging Victorian lamps and many old pictures of the Virginia & Truckee Railroad and early day Reno.

Another large, but still tourist attraction, is The Delta (saloon and restaurant) which started operating in 1876 after the fire and has grown to be the largest in town. The old bar is still the focus of the place, but there are banks of slots, and attached restaurant, some meeting rooms (upstairs) and everything else. The bar at The Delta is shown below.

Bar at The Delta, Virginia City, Photo: By the author.

The third category has a quite restricted membership and includes only serious drinking - establishments. Only three of the current lot qualify: the Washoe Club has a bar, some pool tables, but no slots or hot dogs. It is an old time unadorned drinking place. It also has some old chandeliers, a huge mirror behind the bar, a framed nude and a "winding staircase."[3] Another is the Silver Dollar Pub, located in a (daylight) basement beneath the old Silver Dollar Hotel (now a gift store). This small room is reachable down a steep flight of rickety stairs and is now the

---

3) Several places feature "come-on" attractions—such as an old vault, a wedding chapel, antiques and free museums (such as the red-light museum in Julia Bullette's).

intimate local watering hole catering primarily to the locals; it is not touristic at all (since they can't find it) and is a charming place, also unadorned and unpretentious. The third, a venerable institution in town, is the incomparable Crystal Bar.

The Crystal Bar in Virginia City. Bill Mark's place on "C" Street has been there since the heyday of the Comstock era. Bill's father started bartending in the original location in 1901, moved it to its present location in 1930 and died in 1955, when Bill took over. The place is a direct throwback to the glamour of the Comstock with giant mirrors, oil paintings in heavy gilt frames, three French-cut chandeliers and glassware dating back to the late 1800's. There is also a marble bar, a "mystery" clock and a profusion of framed memorabilia including numerous framed photographs of early day miners and buildings of the Comstock, including many bare chested prize fighters with mustaches, and notable crews of miners complete with old lanterns. There were also a number of venerable orchestrations which would twang and tinkle with great gusto upon the deposit of an appropriate coin. The guest register includes many notable signatures such as Thomas Edison, General (President) Grant and Generals Sheridan and Sherman. Bill is the prototype old time bartender (who even looks the type) whose specialty is mint juleps (in summer) and he and Margaret, his wife, will mingle with the crowd, introduce strangers and give directions.

Above is an early picture (1889) of The Crystal Bar Virginia City: Note the chandelier (still there), the white bar (still there), and the wallpaper (still there). Photo: Nevada Historical Society.

Same bar; different bartender, 1972. Photo: Nevada Historical Society

Some years ago, <u>Time</u> Magazine nominated the <u>Crystal Bar</u> to be one of the ten best bars in the United States.

Same bar, 1985. Postcard.

Bill was a County Commissioner of Storey County for 17 consecutive years and has held practically every other local public office of trust including being the driving fore behind the perpetually winning high school basketball team.

He was born in Virginia City and graduated with the last class in 1936 from the 4th Ward School, served in the Air Force in World War II, and was an active member of at least a dozen organizations.

Bill Marks, bartender – a 1985 photo by the author.

His bar is a remaining vestige of old Nevada as personified by the gandy ebullience of those times. Sometime in the winter especially, Bill would lock the door early especially if the place is full of his friends. This is just the way it is.

Bill died January 12, 1994, the age of 75. His widow, Margaret, still operates (with help) the establishment.

Virginia City also has the distinction of offering the only "brew pub" in Northern Nevada. This is the Union Brewery, on of the oldest buildings in town, having been a brewery from 1862 to 1897. Rick Hoover, owner and brew master, makes about 45 gallons of dark lager beer a week in the basement which is then sold on tap in the saloon upstairs—usually quite rapidly. The place has (very) irregular hours however, and may not be open when you might wish it were.

"C" Street in Virginia City in 1944. Photo: By James Lawrence

TWENTY ONE

OLD SALOONS OF ELKO

Elko began as a railroad camp when the C. P. R. R. reached this point in late 1868.[1] From the beginning it was a rough and tumble place, a volatile mixture of railroad workers, miners, gamblers and a few adventurous merchants. One of the first buildings in this new town was the Cosmopolitan Hotel built in 1869 next to the railroad tracks. It had 80 rooms, a long bar, a cafe, billiard room and a barber shop. This later became the Chamberlain Hotel, and then the Depot Hotel. Between 1869 and 1904 this was the best in town. The original was a frame building with a few bedrooms, a bar and a dining room. Eventually it became a two story brick hotel. It was purchased in 1925 and remodeled to 75 rooms.

In 1869, within a year of Elko's incorporation, there were 22 general stores, two banks, three hardware stores, five lumberyards, ten blacksmiths, four drug stores, eight physicians, eight attorneys and 45 saloons in town, the latter outnumbering all other business categories. Almost all of these were lined up on Commercial Street and included such old names as:

> Gem Saloon (Commercial Street)
> International Saloon (Commercial Street)
> Matt Tracy's Saloon (Commercial Street)
> Gambrinus Saloon (Commercial Street opposite the depot)
> Lager Beer Brewery and Bakery (Commercial Street opposite the depot)
> Ocean Spray Saloon (Commercial Street opposite the lower depot)
> Washoe Saloon (Commercial Street opposite the lower depot)
> Cosmopolitan Saloon (later Depot Hotel)
> White Pine Saloon (6th and Commercial)
> ("The most delicate fancy drinks are compounded by skillful mixologists
> in a style that captivates the public and makes them happy").
> Tuolumine Saloon (between 4th and 5th on Commercial)
> Oyster Bar (fresh oysters in every shape)
> Humboldt Brewery Saloon (5th and Commercial)

Along with the saloons, there were of course – "girls"

> "In numerous houses of prostitution girls sat by red-lighted windows
> along Adobe and Piety Rows, beckoning to cowboys, miners, woodchop-
> pers, teamsters, and gamblers. Ten houses of prostitution, each using
> from six to twenty women, located along Adobe and Piety Rows.[2] One
> house, operated by Mose Haynes (with Belle Wilder as madam), ran in
> conjunction with Haynes' notorious gambling hall. Short, red-haired, red

---

1) The Central Pacific Railroad became the Southern Pacific in 1899.
2) "Elko in 1869 to 90 years later had a red-light district second to none in Nevada and a cheery night life of gunfire, murder and violence in a multiplicity of saloons" Beebe "Central Pacific and Southern Pacific Railroads".

red-whiskered Haynes wore a grin that showed yellow-hued teeth and carried a knife at all times in a scabbard suspended about his neck. Hurdy Gurdy[3] girls ranked a few notches above prostitutes. At Tom Gibbon's Pioneer Saloon (site of present Pioneer Hotel, 5th and Railroad Streets), Sallie Whitmore and her brazen girls flounced about amid whiskey and tumult in the free-wheeling bar and dance hall, enticing men to drink and buy more house drinks." (Nevada's Northeastern Frontier)

Sometime around 1895, Al Fisher's Saloon was a popular drinking spot nearby Wells. The picture below shows a nice front bar and an interesting back bar complete with mirror—and some fancy wallpaper, usual to the time.

Al Fisher's Saloon, Wells, Nevada. Photo: Northeastern Nevada Museum, Elko, Nevada.

In 1904, the Mayer Hotel was constructed, later to become the Stockman's. In 1908 the W. P. R. R. came through town which encouraged a number of "Basque" style Hotels (lodging houses) along Silver Street, such as The Star, The Telescope and The Nevada. The Telescope has long been defunct, however, the other two are thriving. One caters to Spanish Basque, the other to the French variety.

---

3) The name "Hurdy Gurdy" came from the small parlor organ, so common at the time.

The years passed, as did many, if not most, of these early establishments...By 1959 the list had changed and then included:

Club Elko (with dancing)
Lewis Inn (west of town)
The Palm (still there)
Crumley Hotel
Nevada Hotel (on Silver Street – still there)
The Pioneer (now the Overland Bar)
The Stockman's (still there)
The Telescope (now in another use)
Western Inn
Central Cafe
El Dorado
The Star (hotel and restaurant – still active)

Fancy names (for saloons) were nice, but not necessary. Both the Elko Saloon and the Elk Saloon were side by side in early Elko (1905), they exhibit the usual one story wood frame structure with a projecting arcade.

Some of the current interesting saloons in Elko area:

The Silver Dollar (not to be confused with the much newer Silver Dollar Saloon & Casino on Idaho Street) is on the corner of 4th and Commercial Streets. It appears to be rather bare but the usual evening crowd fills it up comfortably. The fine back bar is from Goldfield, originally transported to the Commercial Hotel but installed here in 1934 after prohibition was repealed. The building was originally a bank in 1878, then a store, before its present use. There are a few slots and a number of pool tables in the rear which are often full of young Mexicans, but they are never bothersome.

Back bar at the <u>Silver Dollar</u> – Elko. Photo: By the author.

<u>The</u> <u>Palm</u> This long and narrow bar began operations in 1910 and very little has changed since then. There is a classic hardwood bar and back bar that is an original, as well as a shuffleboard and a few slots (but none are inset into the bar). The pictures on the walls run heavily to prize race horses.

The antique bar at the <u>The Palm</u> – Elko. Photo: By the author.

The <u>Star</u> restaurant and bar on the corner of 3rd and Silver Streets in Elko is perhaps most famous for its food, but the bar is interesting as well, both for the Basque residents of the establishment and the varied people having a picon[4] while waiting to eat. An early Basque pioneer (Pete Jaurequi) built it in 1909 (his heavy iron safe with his name on it is still behind the bar) and it was subsequently operated by the Bengoas, Ozamis and the Sarasuas. It was sold recently to Miguel Leonis and Seviano Lucano, two Basque boys from Gardnerville, who are now the operators.

The bar is rather unpretentious, appearing to be in the "mid-thirties" decor, but the picons are good, the noise level about right and the conviviality comparable to much older "character' oases.

The <u>White Front Bar</u>, in Mountain City[5] (Elko County) was a landmark in that area until 1974, when it was totally destroyed by fire. Built in 1937, it had an old "Brunswick" back bar, a small dance floor and a few gaming tables. Originally catering to miners, it later became a hangout for cowboys and Indians. It was sort of a community center for a vast trading area along the northern Nevada border. The site is now occupied by the post office and a trailer-bar. There were three other saloons in town in those days, including the <u>Red Bar</u>, <u>The Nevada</u> and the <u>Miner's Club</u>; only the <u>Miner's Club</u> remains. There was also a hotel at the time which had a fine restaurant, some gambling, and a bar. It, too, burnt in 1952.

⊰ ⊱

> THE REVOLVER AGAIN–Sunday night a man named Thomas Clay was in a liquor saloon engaged in a social game of cards. Someone came in and told him that a woman wanted to see him outside. He stepped to the door, and as he did so, she caught him by the colar with her left hand and held him while she fired a shot at him with a revovler which she held in her right. A struggle ensued and she fired two more shots. The woman whose name and station we were unable to learn ran away after the third shot. Clay sustained only powder burns
>
> *–April 27, 1871*

---

4) Picon (punch) is a Basque pre-dinner drink which is a mixture of Amer picon, brandy and soda. They are sort of bitter sweet (sometimes called "Basco" cokes) but have a distinct wallop—don't drink more than two.

5) Mountain City began life as Cope in late 1869, by midsummer 1870, it had 20 saloons, one dozen hotels, six restaurants, three lawyers and a "love store."

"Known for its heavy drinkers, Elko lived up to its reputation. Personages such as Ben Yates and Senator Thomas Hunter competed for the first drink of the day. It was the custom in saloons for the first drink of the morning to be "on the house". Senator Hunter and Yates vied with one another for the favor. After starting at Tom Taylor's Saloon at Seventh and Commercial Streets, they enjoyed another drink at Chris Baumback's, and the next was obtained at Jim Gutridge's Elk Saloon. Then they stopped at the Commercial Saloon and "Dad" Shirley's (on the site of the present Nevada Bank of Commerce). The salutation of the day continued at Harelson's Saloon, followed by more imbibing at Reckart's Bar (now the location of First National Bank), and the last drink of the morning was downed at Frank Robinson's Pioneer Saloon. Many fellow townsmen agreed that Senator Tom Hunter could hold more liquor than any man alive, yet no one ever saw him drunk." (Northeast Nevada Frontier)

In 1869 hot sulphur springs about two miles south of Elko, and the Hot Hole springs on the south bank of the Humboldt River below the town, both landmarks along the old emigrant trail, were developed into Laumeister & Groepper's Humboldt Hot Springs spa. Also known as White Sulphur Hot Springs, the hotel and bath-house went through many ownerships and two disastrous fires before 1900. The first fire occurred the night of June 6, 1882, and burned the resort, constructed of wood, to the ground. The second fire occurred at 1:00 A.M. on the morning of June 23, 1899. The bar, apparently, was a great place and a major attraction – but it didn't survive.

Hot Springs barroom – Elko, 1905. Photo: Courtesy of Northeastern Nevada Museum.

TWENTY TWO

SALOONS OF EUREKA

Eureka was found by five prospectors from Austin searching the hills of central Nevada in 1864. It was at first a silver strike, but later proved to be a most important lead/silver discovery.

Founded mainly on silver and lead, (which seems to have less appeal than gold), Eureka grew slowly and steadily, unlike most Nevada mining camps. From 1871 to 1888, this town controlled the lead market nationally. But it had a rough element; it was said that you could hire a man killed for $10 (actually the price was $25). After the completion of the Eureka-Palisade Railroad in October, 1875, Eureka became a wagon and stage center to most of eastern Nevada, growing to be the second largest city in the state at that time, about 9,000 population (1878). The town listed 100 saloons, 25 gambling halls, theatres, newspapers, even an opera house. The town had 10,000 persons at its height with about 8,000 more in Ruby Hill.

The main early saloons were:

> The Tiger (Joe Mendez, proprietor) now the Nevada Club. This place has a notorious reputation for gunfights. It burned in 1880, but was rebuilt.[1]
> The Truckee Saloon
> Lautenschlagers Billiard Hall Owl Club and restaurant—next to the Tiger and still operating under a different name with a nice old bar and adjacent restaurant.
> Gold Bar (and hotel) Stone Saloon
> San Francisco Brewery
> Brawn and Godfrey's Oyster Saloon
> The Corner Located on the corner of Clark and Main Streets, this was said to be the "finest saloon in all Nevada." In later years it carried a different name and then became a Bank in the late 1930's.
> Palace Saloon

Present day Eureka still has a few interesting holdover saloons, notably the Owl Club. This building was originally a two story structure with a brewery downstairs and a saloon upstairs. After the great fire of 1880, the top floor was removed and the lower floor established as a saloon, which it has been ever since.

---

1) "This saloon has been fitted up with a view to comfort unsurpassed by any saloon establishment in Nevada. To a stranger it is a perfect mystery. Upstairs and down, turn as you will you always find yourself before a bar, supplied with the finest brands of wines, liquors and cigars. Experienced and attentive bartenders are always on hand to serve patrons of the house. San Jose, Frederick beers constantly on draft. Also English Porter, German wine, St. Louis Beer, Milwaukee Beer and the celebrated Culmback Beer on tap." Early ad for The Tiger.

Eureka Saloons (and whore houses) were sorely tested in 1918 when the manager of the Eureka Nevada Railroad, a major economic force in the area, decreed one day (most unexpectedly) that: "I will make no effort to run any trains until the people of Eureka stand in with us and clean up. If the saloons are left running, we will have nothing but turmoil. Let the saloons lay off six months or a year and then by petition, if they promise to be half way decent, they may be permitted, if you see fit, to pollute the laboring man further."

There is no written record of what finally became of all of this—but the saloons are still there.

Railroad Saloon and Store,

JOSEPH VANINA, Proprietor.

ALL KINDS OF MERCHANDISE CONSTANTLY ON HAND.

COAL CONTRACTING A SPECIALTY.

Main Street,   Eureka, Nev.

PALACE SALOON,

UP STAIRS IN H. VORBERG'S BUILDING, MAIN ST.

The Choicest Brands of Wines, Liquors and Cigars.

POOL AND BILLIARDS.

☞ ELEGANTLY FURNISHED CLUB ROOMS.

LUTHER CLARK & CO., Proprietors.

JACK PERRY'S

COURT HOUSE EXCHANGE.

Corner Main and Bateman Streets, Eureka, Nev.

The Choisest Wines, Liquors & Cigars

Obtainable in the San Francisco Market constantly on hand.

THE TIGER,

JOS. MENDES, PROPRIETOR.

This saloon has been fitted up with a view to comfort, unsurpassed by any similar establishment in the State. To a stranger it is a perfect mystery. Up stairs and down, turn as you will, you always find yourself before a bar, supplied with the choicest brands of **Wines, Liquors and Cigars.** Experienced and attentive bar-keepers are always on hand to serve the patrons of the House. San Jose Fredricksburg Beer constantly on draught. Also XXX English Porter, German Wine, St. Louis Beer, Milwaukee Beer, and the celebrated Culmbach Beer on tap.

<u>Owl Club</u> 1991. Photo: By the author.

TWENTY THREE

OLD SALOONS OF TONOPAH

Tonopah (an Indian word meaning "waterbrush") began in 1900 when a prospector accidently found worthwhile pay rock. An immediate rush began and a "tent town" swiftly ensued.

By only the fall of 1902 Tonopah had increased to over 3,000 persons with faro games, two dance halls, three banks, three water companies, three bakeries, 60 saloons, a brewery and foundry and a two block red-light district.

Tonopah by 1907 had become a major Nevada community with five banks, several hotels, numerous cafes, gambling palaces, several schools, and three newspapers. It had become the center of a large and growing midstate mining area including such places as Goldfield, Bullfrog, Rawhide, Manhattan, Round Mountain and Belmont.

Tonopah offered a plenitude of gambling and drinking 24 hours a day. Gambling in those days meant table games since slots hadn't been invented. Ritch's Saloon, on the ground floor in the back of the Brokers Exchange Building was perhaps the fanciest place in town; there players bet ten dollar gold pieces at will on a variety of games of chance. The Tonopah Club was the largest and busiest saloon however.

Main Street, Tonopah. Photo: Carlos Morales.

The Mizpah Hotel and Bar, on the corner of Main and Brougher Streets in Tonopah has always been important. The first building where the Mizpah now stands was the Mizpah Saloon, a framed building with a bar and grill erected in June, 1901, only a year after the initial discovery. It was a lively spot even though somewhat rough in appearance and function. The town rapidly outgrew it and by 1905 it was moved to the edge (then) of town and replaced by the (then) largest building in town, which housed the Tonopah Banking Corporation, as well as real estate, mining, and some law firms, and also served as a hotel. It was constructed from granite from nearby Mt. Brougher and was, and is, known as the Mizpah Annex. A new hotel – at a cost of $200,000 was begun with a grand opening on the 17th of November, 1908 (although the upper stories were not finished until later). It was equipped with the, "finest oak furnishings, the most ornate fixtures, the latest in modern indoor conveniences and huge plate glass windows on the first floor", as well as electric elevators. It immediately became the center of town – and still is.

Bars have always been the major social center for Tonopah citizenry. The largest and grandest was the Big Casino (then known as the "Monte Carlo of Nevada"), which opened in April, 1915. It included a restaurant, saloon, betting hall, and dance floor. It was "the largest hurdy-gurdy house on the east coast." In August 1922 it was destroyed by fire, which also razed the entire lower end of town.

By the late 1930's economic activity in Tonopah had sunk to new lows, but there were still more than a dozen bars and brothels operating. These included such names as: Silver State Bar, Effie's Place, Taxcines Bar, The Lucky Strike, Fay's Place, The Bungalow, Newport Dance Hall, The Green Lantern, The Northern (of course), Cottage Bar, Parker Place and Nigger Dee (The mix ran heavily in favor of brothels).

Tonopah loved parades. These festive occasions provided flags of all nations, uniformed bandsmen and grand attires. Sometimes there were more people in the parade than watching it. Photo: Nevada Highway Magazine.

~ TWENTY FOUR ~

OLD SALOONS
OF THE EASTERN FRONTIER

The far easterly edge of Nevada, abutting the state of Utah is a somewhat isolated area with few very widely separated old and small towns, all of which date back to the turn of the century. Most are related to mining activities (McGill, Ely, Ruth, Pioche), although there are some founded on agricultural interests such as Panaca, and Alamo.

Ely, the largest community in the area has little to offer from an old saloon standpoint. There are a few local bars in town, but none of them fit to the category.

Pioche, about 110 miles south of Ely, is an early town of the Comstock era, beginning in 1869. During the 1870's it was recognized as one of the wildest mining camps of the far west; it is said that the local boot hill had 75 graves before someone finally died of natural causes. The town is on a State Highway, but has recently been bypassed by another more convenient route and this with the closing of the mines, has resulted in a diminished economy and population, now down to about 750 persons. There are, however, three remaining bars in town, just a shadow of the 72 which served it in earlier times. The two oldest are the Overland Hotel and Bar and The Alamo, both dating from the 1880's. The Overland Bar features an 1864 Brunswick Bar built in England with a cherry wood front bar and mahogany back bar, once in a saloon in Kimberly. The present saloon began in 1940, although the building dates back 120 years. There are slots, a 21 table, old lamps, pictures and animal heads, as well as a dance floor. The Alamo was erected in 1864, operated in the mid – 1880's as a bank, but later was converted back to a bar when the present back bar was imported from Salt Lake City some 60 years ago. This back bar features large square columns with ionic capitals; the large mirror, so often a basic feature, has been painted over with a lurid and insipid landscape which is "framed" by rough bark, a totally incongruous situation. Here also are a few slots, a pool table, a 21 table and juke box. The third bar in town is The Nevada Club, which opened after the repeal of Prohibition, about 1933.

Panaca, a few miles south, and nearby Alamo, have no saloons at all – a fact directly related to the strong Mormon influence in these towns.

But Caliente, first known as Dutch Flat and settled in the 1870's, is still a drinking town, although here too, the many earlier watering places have shrunk to just three. Two of these are routine, however, Rex Esley's Shamrock Club, opening in 1945, has roots that go back to 1900. None of the three really qualify as an old Nevada Saloon, although the level of camaraderie is high in several of them.

In its earlier years, however, Caliente was a more roaring place with a few outstanding "roaring places." Two of these are still somewhat famous. One was the old San Pedro dating from the beginning of town but now part of a store, and the second was The Gardens, which during prohibition (1929) advertised "Rootbeer on tap – a gentlemen's resort where your pleasure is our motto." There was also Bucket of Blood Saloon in those days, but little is known of it.

For the last 80 years or so, Caliente has been a strong railroad town, which undoubtedly has contributed to the longevity of the saloon scene.

Old San Pedro in Caliente (now gone)

The stand out saloon of this eastern frontier is, without doubt, the McGill Club Inc. in McGill. This almost deserted hamlet, some 12 miles north of Ely in White Pine County, was once a major copper producer were the Kennecott Smelter provided copper bars around the clock, employing a large number of miners. But the mines closed, the mill shut down, the employees left and now there are only a few desultory vacant store fronts…and the McGill Club. The Copper Club next door, also a saloon mainstay in years past, is now the post office.

The long bar, originally constructed on the east coast and shipped (in three sections) around the horn and then by train to Caliente, was eventually freighted by wagon to East Ely in 1907 to grace The Antler Bar there, but was moved to McGill in 1910. The building has seen a variety of uses including a trucking company in 1909, a grocery store before prohibition and then a barber shop during that period (with a flourishing speakeasy in back). Norman Linnell, who started working the club in 1937 when he was only 15 years old is still there. Until recently he was aided by "Suzy" Symes who also began there young – he was swamping out the place while still in grade school.

The back bar at the McGill Club, McGill, Nevada, taken from an old postcard.

World War II produced a unique entrance display – an array of floor to ceiling photographs of about 300 McGill G.I.'s, they are still there – 50 years later.

There is a dance floor and a juke box and some slot machines, but it is still primarily a drinking bar. And well worth the 12 mile detour.

Exterior view of the <u>McGill Club</u> in McGill, 1991. Cyprus was the name of the private railroad car belonging to the president of the mining company. Old postcard.

McGill was, from the beginning, a Company Town created by the Steptoe Valley Mining and Smelting Company who erected a smelter here in 1906 in order to utilize the water from Duck Creek. It was named after a rancher in the area. By 1920 the town had grown larger than Ely, but in July, 1922 a major fire all but wiped it out. Three smaller satellite "sin towns" clustered nearby – all on private property and not subject to McGill's control. These were Smelterville, Ragdump and Steptoe City. All were rife with saloons, dance halls, gambling dens and cribs catering to the miners from McGill who were denied such activities in their own community. All are now long gone – faded from even the memories of today's White Pine residents.

THE "FLACK DRUNK"

The ready availability of saloons exerted some strange influences in some strange ways in early Nevada. One example is that of John Flack. John Flack, an attorney, appeared in Elko in 1869 at the very beginning of the town. Born in Kentucky, raised in Missouri, he, like many others, succumbed to the spell of gold in California. But he arrived a bit too late; the big rush was over. Lawyering wasn't too profitable so he backtracked to Nevada settling in Washoe Valley. It wasn't much better there either, and hearing of "White Pine Fever," he headed for Elko. The City had just been formed legally, and although not yet a registered voter, Democrat Flack ran for District Judge, barely losing this first attempt by only 14 votes. In 1870 at the regular election he ran again (presumably registered by now) and won—a post he held until his death.

He was involved in several sensational trials. The first was the case of the "Montello Robbers"—for train robbery. He also presided over the trail of Josiah and Elizabeth Potts for murder, resulting in the first and only woman to be executed for murder in the State of Nevada.

His courtroom manner was rather informal to say the least. He had little regard for his personal appearance and often presided with huge patches in his trousers. He frequently dozed through important testimony, but worst of all, he periodically went on what was locally called a "Flack Drunk."

This involved first exchanging a silver dollar for ten dimes. He would then visit ten saloons, ordering one drink at each in turn. While drinks were really "two bits" in those days, the bartenders always poured a double, and accepted his dime: after all he was The Judge. Whoever happened to be around at the last saloon would help him home.

Surprisingly, his decisions were seldom overruled by the Supreme Court.

He died in September, 1891, at the age of 44 and is buried in Elko. His funeral was a grand affair, attended a large retinue of friends and county officials.

TWENTY FIVE

OLD SALOONS IN CARSON VALLEY

Carson Valley, in Douglas County, nestled against the Sierra escarpment, was the first settled area in Nevada. Its resultant long history included the establishment and operation of a number of notable drinking places, some of which have disappeared – See Chapter Five – Five Defunct Saloons of Douglas, but some of which are still active. Most of these remaining saloons exhibit a eclectic mixture of clientele ranging from ranchers (in rubber irrigation boots), cowboy types (real or imagined), local businessmen and idle retired widows playing nickel slots, to the ubiquitous tourist – sometimes waiting to be seated in the adjoining restaurant, sometimes on a brief rest stop between busses and sometimes down from Tahoe for a day in the country. Regardless, they all find the saloons of Carson Valley most interesting. Some of them are:

Valley Bar. This small one story old wood structure at the intersection of State Route 88 and Centerville Lane is about all that is left of the earlier town of Centerville when Carson Valley was an agrarian community and people didn't travel long distances for anything. Known as the "Pride of the West," the bar which might seat about nine or ten offers only a standard fare with no frills. There is no glitter, no nude painting, no "class" – just the honest workingman's establishment catering to nearby ranchers and the construction trade. It is a social center and an interesting place to while away a snowy evening. Beer is the usual drink here, but everything is available.

Valley Bar. Photo: By the author.

J/T Bar (and Restaurant) in Gardnerville, is an old establishment and a redolent voice from the past. Home to the "Big Swede" in its earlier years, it was moved to this location from its original site in Virginia City in 1895 (where it was then a bagnio). This "French" Basque bar (not be confused with the "Spanish" –Basque bar–the Overland, across the street, is owned and operated by the Lukemberry family, is still a true community center gathering place and still caters to the "old Nevadan" mainly from Carson Valley, but also Smith and Mason Valleys as well. Curing the summer there are a number of tourists from Lake Tahoe. The 12 foot ceiling is covered with folded paper money which is thrown up there by Jean using a special trick which he has developed over the years. Jean is also quite knowledgeable on political affairs and is always willing to discuss and argue (always politely) the National, State, or local issue of the day. It is a "character" place and really hasn't changed much in the last 50 years. Jeano (as he was called) was found dead at the age of 68, behind his beloved bar on August 9, 1993. He was, of course, wearing his ever present black beret.

J/T Bar and Restaurant in Gardnerville in 1991. The portico is gone (unfortunately) and the top floor is the barber shop otherwise it is much the same. Photo: Scott Smith.

The Overland, on the other side of the Main Street was, until recently, operated by Eusubio Ceñoz who came to this country from Spain in 1954 at 29 years of age is also a bar and a (Basque) restaurant. He immediately became a sheepherder in the Twin Lakes area in adjacent California near Bridgeport, (on his way to that region he had his first meal in Nevada – at the Overland). For 12 years he tended sheep in the Sierra. He then moved to the Gerlach-Eagleville area in April, 1961, spent some time in Alturas, but in 1966 returned to become a cook at the J & T. In 1967, he leased the Overland and in 1972 brought the premises from the Etchemendys was had operated the place for over 50 years, having acquired the building in 1921. The building was originally constructed in 1911, and featured a butcher shop in the rear as well as 12 hotel rooms upstairs. In 1980, Eusebio brought his new wife, Elvira, also a true Basque, from the Alturas (California) area into the operation.

Eusubio died in 1989. Elvira is carrying along the spirit of the place with style, service and great food, which often features lamb with an emphasis on garlic.

Interior of the Overland Hotel and Bar about 1922. Photo: Courtesy Elvira Ceñoz.

The French: Operated in the early days by Baptiste Borda, originally another sheepman, he purchased the adjoining I.O.O.F. Building in 1935, remodeling it into the Glock Grocery Store. He leased the building on December 1, 1937, then died suddenly on December 14, 1937 in Dayton, at the age of 41.. Raymond Borda continued operations for many more years. It is a popular spot for construction workers and baseball players.

Exterior – French Bar on main street in Gardnerville. Photo: By the author (1991).

Interior – French Bar - 1991. Photo: By Bret Duster.

Pony Express, the modern "Pony Express", formerly the early Heidelberg (see pages 27-28) is also again operating, however, it has been completely redone inside with pecky cedar which adds nothing to enhance its historic character. The exterior is much the same however (however it is now being remodeled again).

Other old time saloons in Carson Valley include of course the "oldest bar" – the Genoa Bar (see page 39) which is in a class by itself.

TWENTY SIX

NEVADA SALOONS
AND PROHIBITION

Premonitions of disaster over took the saloon trade in 1920 when prohibition went into effect. Many, if not most of the Nevada saloons, continued to operate however and to prosper through a variety of diversified and often nefarious means.

Prohibition – American's greatest failure, is still remembered as a time when law breaking was the most popular game in the land. This unnatural state lasted until December 5, 1933 when the 18th Amendment was repealed and once again the role of drinking and the Nevada saloon assumed it true importance.

Scene in Reno in October 1920, the night before Prohibition took effect.
Photo: Courtesy of Marshall Fey.

On the first day of Prohibition the Elko Independent editor reported, "This is sure a quiet town today. Nobody arrested, nobody dead, nobody married, nobody drunk, nobody gone away, nobody home, nobody robbed, nobody licked, no fights, no fires, no calamities. Thank Heaven! But it's a poor heaven for the newspaper man."

Prohibition, for the most part, was a big joke in Nevada. The state was small (in population), extremely rural in character, quite rugged in disposition and almost everyone knew each other. There were many convenient places, some even close to the main population centers, in which to hide a still[1] and the people were just independent enough not to care too much for this recent eastern wild idea. After all, in 1920 there were many grizzled Nevadans who had lived through the hard years in Tonopah, Marietta, or Austin, and who were extremely self reliant, and knowledgeable as to the makings of various potent brews, or at least where a bottle might quickly be found.

Many saloons quickly became "soft drink" emporiums.[2] These two-faced clubs thrived openly throughout the state. On the one side the establishment maintained a soft drink palace, while behind a "peek-a-boo" door on the other side a "speakeasy" functioned for the many who were "wets." Card games, which were illegal in the state, also flourished in these hidden rooms.

The local police usually regarded enforcement quite lightly and left the task to the Federal officers – called "prohi's." As might be expected, they were about as popular as rattlesnakes. Even many dedicated "drys" could not sympathize with a person whose only mission in life was to shut down illegal gin mills. Their popularity was not enhanced by the fact that all funds collected for fines – on conviction – went into the Federal coffers; local police got nothing. In the protective isolation of much of rural Nevada, prohibition didn't stand much of a chance, although some establishments were temporarily (usually very temporarily) shut down for dispensing bootleg booze.

In the towns, though, there was some effort by the Feds to control things. Robert Laxalt, in his recent book, The Basque Hotel, concerning growing up in Carson City, mentions these influences in that small community. Most early day saloons continued to operate, either by increased activity "out the back door" (such as Jack's Bar in Carson for instance) or by proclaiming to substitute "root beer" – as was the case in Caliente, nor could anyone entirely buck the flow of booze through so-called "hip peddlers." Nevertheless, it was a great day in December, 1933 when it was finally and legally ended. New Year's Eve that year was a three day orgy even though it rained most of the time.

In the early 1920's just after the enactment of prohibition an air mail pilot became lost and had to crash land in a remote part of northern Elko county. Since communication was sort of spotty, after a few days he was given up for lost. But then he walked into a ranch and asked for a ride to town.

It developed that after the landing he had been held prisoner by some moonshiners operating in these hidden canyons who saw the U. S. markings on the plane and concluded that he was a "prohi" out looking for stills. Apparently he did alot of fast talking and some successful convincing while looking down the barrels of several shotguns.

---

1) Abandoned mines for instance, which were plentiful, were ideal for this purpose. Pahrump Pyrrenes, near Las Vegas was notorious for "a considerable production of illegal booze.".

2) One Ely *Daily Times* story reflected the casual attitude: "Ely is included in a list of Nevada communities where federal padlocks will close "soft drink" emporiums that have come under Uncle Sam's ban for selling 'white mule' which officials have decided carries too much of a wallop to be classified as strictly temperance drinks."

TWENTY SEVEN

SOME LITTLE KNOWN SALOONS
(OLD AND NEW)

In travels around the State over the years, it has been my good fortune to become acquainted with a number of rural bars which still have (some of) the classic attributes of early Nevada saloons. A few stand out as being exemplary modern day direct descendants of the old Nevada saloon in its purest sense. Unfortunately, not all of them are still in operation, but those who are not are remembered and mourned with fondness. Some of those still operating are:

Bruno's (Country Club) Bar in Gerlach. Gerlach is a very remote community at the end of the Granite Range, separating the Smoke Creek Black Rock and Granite Creek Deserts in Northern Washoe County. It was, and still is a tough town, frequented by miners, cowboys and railroaders, but it's that remoteness and setting which tends to preserve the elements of an earlier day Nevada town. While not (at all) fitting the typical physical description of the early Nevada Bar, this establishment meets all of the social criteria for being the core of this community. A somewhat utilitarian structure with a nondescript appearance, with now a small cafe attached, it is the newer version of Bruno's older bar which burned down in 1982. Bruno is, of course, the star attraction since he is responsible solely for its initiation and success (and now owns almost everything else in Gerlach) as well as being a "character" in his own right. The clientele ranges from miners from the nearby Empire Gypsum operation, to railroaders (the Western Pacific Main Line runs through town), to ranchers, to hunters (in season), to the more permanent residents, who seem to be there continually. The conversations, especially late at night, are wide ranging and provocative. The atmosphere is convivial and the rowdiness minimal, although there is some, usually minor knife fights between the Mexican gandy dancers sometimes. There is nothing taking place in this vast area that Bruno doesn't know about. He is a storehouse of vital information, ranging from where to hunt chukkers to who is ill, better or worsening. This is the veritable epitome of the common gathering place; the very essence of the original Nevada saloon.

Waterhole #1 - Located in Golconda (not to be confused with the Water'n Hole bar in Pahrump). This is a side-of-the-road local gathering place in the old small town tradition. While considerably non-descriptive, it is interesting in that it caters only to the local citizenry, and the current (and past) local citizenry are a colorful and independent bunch indeed. It was the locale of the now famous escapade of a few years back involving a pig. Get someone sitting next to you at the bar to tell you about it.

The Cutthroat Saloon in Markleeville (actually in Alpine County in California) but otherwise a totally Nevada type institution. This large two story building doubles as a restaurant, but the bar is the gathering place for the area and a fun place at all times, especially after 10:00 P.M. During the fall hunting season the place is packed and the motorcycle clubs from all over Northern California seem to find it irresistible during all parts of the year.

The Cutthroat Saloon.
Photo: By the author.

The Central Bar in Smith Valley is still a local gathering place with a distinct old fashioned aura.
Photo: By the author.

CG Bar: in Wellington is located on the far west side of Smith Valley in Lyon County. This purely local bar (and restaurant) was very popular with the area's growing population and often served as a sort of "Community Hall" for gatherings of all kinds. Unfortunately, it burnt to the ground in the spring of 1991, was rebuilt and then burned again, it is (again) now being rebuilt.

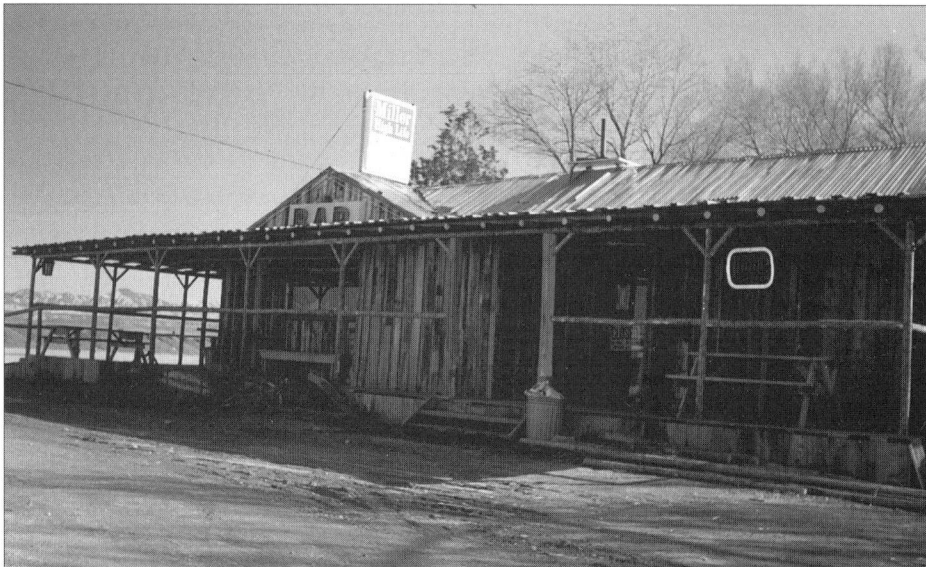

The Middlegate Bar, at the intersection of U. S. 50 and the road south to Gabbs has long been a "central" place for a huge, but sparsely populated area of central Nevada. It was closed when I last stopped by however.
Photo: By the author.

Jiggs Bar in Jiggs[1] (Elko County), another remote structure some 33 miles south of Elko on the road to Ruby Marshes is the town; which otherwise includes only the elementary school, a large two story brick mansion and a mobile home for the school teacher. Many years ago it acquired a small measure of fame when all of its inhabitants were stuffed into a VW van, which was advertised nationally. It is still an interesting place and a convenient stop between Elko and the fishing at the Ruby Marshes. The bar itself is a low ceilinged, somewhat rickety structure with a veritable "museum" of interesting things to look at. Ranchers, cowboys and fishermen are its stable support.

Early picture of the Jiggs Saloon, then called Hylton. Photo: Northeast Nevada Museum.

1) The Jiggs Bar has a long history. Originally known as Dry Creek from 1874 to 1879, it then became Round Valley (1879-1881), then Skelton (1884 to 1911), changing to Hylton from 1911 to 1913, and finally to Jiggs, since 1918. In the early 1900's the community boasted a hotel, community buildings, school, saloon and old-fashioned general store, a number of dwellings and about 35 people.

The Branding Iron Bar in Fernley is also a throwback to an earlier, less complicated day. This ramshackle building, near the Fallon Road is a hangout for a growing retinue of retirees, sprinkled with workmen from the nearby cement plant plus, of course, the usual "cowboys and Indians."

Branding Iron Bar in Fernley. Photo: By the author (1992).

The Taylor Canyon Club is another remote but interesting saloon located about 35 miles north of Elko on the Independence Valley Road near the turnoff to Tuscarora. This somewhat nondescript wood frame station offers conviviality and a meeting place for a large area of still viable cattle ranches scattered throughout Independence Valley and Jacks Creek country, although with the recent advent of many major gold mining activities in this region, there are now also numerous bearded men with hard hats and beer bottles as well, speaking a language only they seem to understand.

Schellbourne Bar, in Schellbourne, located 43 miles north of Ely in White Pine County features an old bar which once graced The Capitol Club in Ely before it burned in a fire in the late 1940's. An interesting place, but unfortunately not always open, especially when you fervently wish it were. Schellbourne was first a pony express stop, then a stage station, then a fort and eventually a short-lived mining town.

Belmont Saloon: Belmont, the original county seat of Nye County, lies in a wooded canyon about 18 miles northeast of Tonopah. (A paved road most of the way). Long an almost totally deserted ghost town, (in the truest sense) it is now home to a dozen or so new families with modern well built homes and some trailers.

This local bar, the only commercial venture in the community, epitomizes the theme of the bar as the local center of activity. The bar, salvaged from the now collapsed Cosmopolitan Saloon up the street, is quite small, and is in a wooden building which looks older than it is. Inside it features the usual fascinating collection of rustic junk. There is even a (somewhat) – naked lady painting over the bar (see photo) and "T" shirts as well.

Interior of the <u>Belmont Saloon</u>. Photo: By the author.

<u>Hawthorne</u>: The main drinking establishment in town is the El Capitan, which is also the main eating and gaming place as well. There are still several older places on the main street; the biggest and best is <u>Joe's</u> <u>Tavern</u>, operated by Joe Viani Jr. It is a cavernous place, complete with pool tables, rusty metal and dusty photos, plus a small stage. This is a favorite place for the Indians from Schurz, especially after paydays-be careful in here after 9 P.M. on those nights.

Louis and Mary Dotson's <u>The</u> <u>Hideaway</u>: in Wendover is a unique and somewhat hidden, long time restaurant south of the Railroad tracks in a residential area known as Scobieville. It became popular with Air Force personnel from the Wendover AFB, but others, even from Elko go there to shoot pool and dance to a juke box. The house specialty since 1974 is charbroiled steaks. The ambience is undeniable and it is a character place, worth the visit even though it is not an old Nevada saloon in the true sense of the word, since it is now really more of a casino – and called that.

During Prohibition, Oscar Foreman, an old Nevada of the pioneer ilk, had an active still in Newark Valley (in eastern Nevada). His product was good and in due time became somewhat famous, even on the coast, both in San Francisco and Los Angeles. When a prospective customer in these towns specified "Oscar Foreman" he was not only admitted instantly into the back room, but was also recognized as a connoisseur of good moonshine.

The Long Branch Saloon, in Luning, Nevada, is probably the last place you would expect to find a bar of any kind. This one, operating in Luning, with all of 48 permanent residents-is out of the book. Dick, the present owner and bartender is ex-navy (and much of the discussion is navy talk) who has been here almost 20 years. The ceilings are low and leak when it rains (thankfully it seldom does); inside the place is full of "things" ranging from rusty mining paraphernalia to airplane models; the outside is most unpretentious. But it is "character" all the way and a very convenient stop between Hawthorne and points south (no parking problems of course). There is also a shady rest stop across the highway. It does not attract attention; most people don't even slow down-but this is real rural Nevada.

The Long Branch in Luning. Photo: By the author.

The Water'n Hole in Pahrump, in southern Nye County boasts an 1869 Brunswick bar also brought around the horn in a sailing ship. It survived the 1906 earthquake and fire (in San Francisco) and eventually found its way to Elko and then Pahrump (in 1963). This Saloon widely advertised "if you have nothing to do – do it here."

Originally a somewhat decrepit typical desert wooden building called the Cotton Pickin' Saloon, it has been in operation since the early 1960's. During its early days it was the local gathering place for all of the area pioneers; it is now patronized mostly by the many new retiree locals. There is a newer restaurant next door.

Gabbs: This totally isolated "company" town, almost midstate in Nye County, is some 30 miles east of Luning, which in turn is hardly anywhere to begin with. The some 300 people still living there enjoy clean air, no traffic and a simple life which is amply sustained by the two local saloons:

R & D's Bar, in the center of town is sort of plain (inside and out) with a few pool tables, some tables and chairs and no slots, but it is a very friendly place and definitely a local center of the social scene. Several hours imbibing draft beers there one afternoon resulted in some (strange) new friendships - one with "weird" Harold (that's how he introduced himself), the other - "Bill - the blue nun." Both are retired desert rats. Somehow they made the place more fun.

Photo: By the author.

The other place is the Keystone - a large barn like structure on the edge of town. It features a huge wood stove and a very long bar. This is really more of a roadhouse - but equally friendly.

J/S Bar is in Paradise Valley some 40 miles north of Winnemucca at the base of the Santa Rosa Mountains. This old saloon, built in 1910, is the social center of this agricultural community as well as serving hunters, campers, and fisherman (in season). It is open year round, and also offers gas, a pool table and a welcome fire place.

Diamond Bar: In Denio, is about the only business in that town athwart the Oregon border. The place caters to the ranchers, miners, cowboys, rock hounds and some tourists. The facility itself isn't much but it is a friendly place and there is no parking problem. "Howard" (Murran) who ran the place for 50 years (1951 to 1981) was known as a real character.

The Exchange Club: In Beatty, occupies a prominent corner where Highways US 395 makes an abrupt turn. It is a busy place, especially at noon time and on weekends when a heavy influx of both locals and travelers infiltrate the place. Beatty is not only a midpoint between Tonopah and Las Vegas, but is also the turnoff to Death Valley. The Club has operated continuously since it opened in 1906, although at times it has also been a courtroom, city hall, hotel, even a theater. It is built of solid adobe.

The bar, in front, is long and distinguished, with appropriate mirrors and the like. The cafe on the other end is a fast and efficient food service, but sometimes overpowers the "bar part."

Lovelock, usually considered to be a quiet (and somewhat dull) agricultural town, had its share of saloons. In the earlier days a row of them lined Broadway, abutting the railroad tracks, but these have now dwindled to two. These remaining old style Nevada bars include "Walk's Place," and The Ranch House.

Hidden in the historic (but little known) town of Jarbidge, about 100 miles north of Elko, the Outdoor Inn is a magnet for hunters, fishermen explorers and the occasional "lost" tourist. The place is friendly, very friendly and, in fact, is sometimes rowdy. Graffiti covers the walls and ceiling and a hand carved bar runs nearly the length of the room. The sign on the wall tells it all:

"JARBIDGE WILL GET YOU THROUGH TIMES OF NO MONEY BETTER THAN MONEY WILL GET YOU THROUGH TIMES OF NO JARBIDGE."

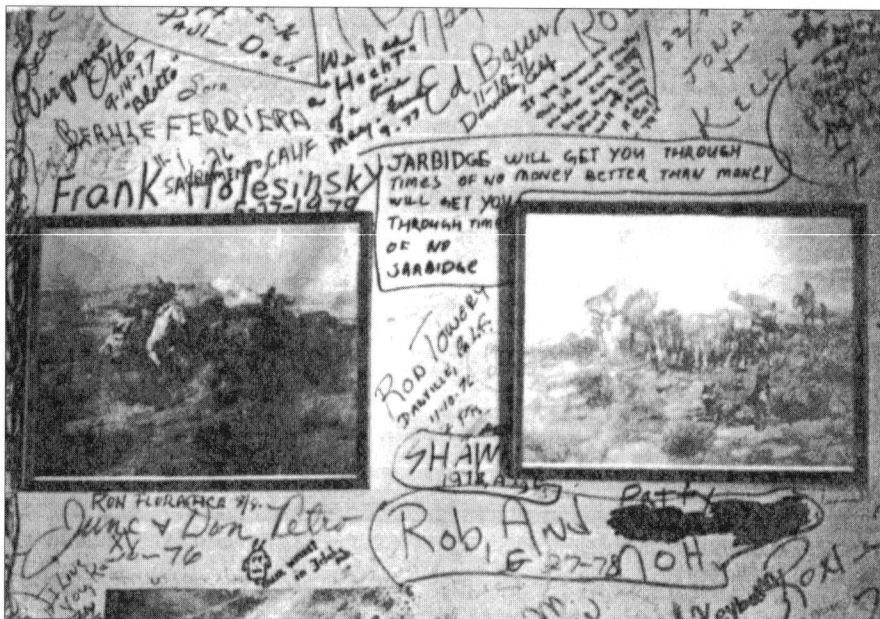

Graffiti inside the remote Outdoor Inn, Jarbidge. Photo: Nevada Magazine.

The other saloon in Jarbidge is the Red Dog, just up the dirt street. With two saloons and a permanent population of less than twenty, this town probably has the most bars per capita of any place in the state. This old frame building has been there for some time. The porch is quite comfortable on hot summer days and the beers are always "ice cold" – as the sign says.

Manhattan: This old "ghost town" has (somewhat) come back to life as a direct result of the mining boom now underway at Round Mountain, a few miles to the north. Situated in a shallow canyon, both Upper and Lower Manhattan once served its own thriving mining endeavors (there is still a big operation in the lower canyon area). Although there are no visible commercial structures there are still two operating bars which serve the liquid needs of the local population. The "upper" canyon establishment—The Manhattan—(without a visible sign) is a turn of the century one room affair, with that usual porch, assorted junk, wagon wheels and leftover mining machinery scattered about. The building itself is rather plain, however, besides drinking, one can play pool, cards or peruse the "library?" Occasionally there is live music and dancing. Entertainment tends to be creative in Manhattan and "celebrations" are impromptu and frequent. One distinctive attraction called "The Chicken Shit." There is an eight by eight foot cage outside, the bottom of which is marked off into 100 spaces. On notable occasions[2] these numbers are

---

(2) Which can be anytime.

~ 124 ~

"bought" by the thirsty patrons for one or two bucks apiece and, when sold out, a live chicken is dropped therein. Whatever number the chicken shits on, is the winner of the pot. Such is life in the Nevada outback!

The Lower area centers on the Miner Saloon (as pictured), a very similar outlet, - but without the chickens.[3]

Miners Saloon at Manhattan. Photo: By the author.

There are a few others which "almost" qualify. These include the Midas Bar[4] (in Midas), the Say When in McDermitt, the Heyday in Smith Valley, the Montgomery Pass Bar on U. S. Highway 6 (on the road from (Coaldale to Bishop) and Carver's Station in the center of Smokey Valley on Highway 376. There may be a few more in southern Nevada.

Time does take its toll. Unfortunately there are a number of good old saloons that once provided a service to their community and qualified as "OLD NEVADA SALOONS" that are gone, probably for good. Following is a somewhat wistful remembrance of some of these:

Ore House in Ione. This funky old one story building is Ione (almost) and a more typical place would be hard to find. Catering to a huge (but sparsely populated) region extending down the Reese River Valley, the Ione Valley, and as far as Gabbs, this old bar was in the traditional form— plank on one side, gaming (and a pool table) on the other. But it is the people who made it. On any day one could find wind bitten ranchers, hard rock miners, truckers, geologists and adventurers, but only a few "tourists," since this place is really remote and only reachable by dirt roads. The saloon wasn't fancy, far from it, but was a gathering place in all the old Nevada tradition. And, in that tradition, everything took place there from a huge family 4th of July celebration featuring free food (and games) to occasional wakes and weddings.

---

(3) Every day or two during the past two weeks large crowds have collected in the rear of the St. Charles Saloon, and have enjoyed rare sport in shooting at chickens furnished for the occasion by the enterprising proprietor of that establishment, Jack Holmes. Pistols were generally used, distance sixty yards, and some excellent shooting has been done. *Reese River Reveille*, January 5, 1864.

(4) Now closed.

The famous Ore House Saloon in Ione – while still operating – 1987. Photo: By the author.

A half mile north of Spanish Ranch on the highway through Independence Valley (in Elko County) under a half dead tree stood the Bucket of Blood Saloon. It operated successfully from 1910 to 1920 and became the center for "everything" in the valley. It functioned as a true community center – a basic role of the frontier saloon.

Tuscarora Tavern: Also in northern Elko County, Tuscarora is now almost a ghost town, but once it was flourishing mining community with a distinct character all its own. In its heyday, during the 1880's, it had its fair share of notable drinking parlors, including such favorites as:

> Idaho Saloon
> Crystal Peak Brewer Depot
> The Delta Saloon
> The Empire Saloon
> Blue Wing Saloon
> and Tuscarora Brewery Hall

There were many others who were too small, too cheap or not inclined, to advertise.

Until recently there was one (only) surviving saloon in this small community—the Tuscarora Tavern. But it is now closed. While it lasted though it won almost a universal reputation. The big iron doors opened promptly at six; the posted closing hour was 10 P.M., but that was seldom observed. All official holidays (and many that were unofficial) were scrupulously observed. There were free lunches (sometimes), eight ball tournaments (sometimes), and all sorts of other shenanigans. It was a sorry day indeed when this rural gem closed.

Photo: Courtesy of Northeast Nevada Museum.

Golden Gate Bar in Silver City: Often, if not always, the character and success of a small town bar is coincidently dependent upon the character of the owner and the bartender. This is true of most of the Basque bars and especially so in the outlying small communities where the clientele is established, familiar and regular. The Golden Gate Bar in Silver City was (it is closed now) a distinct case in point. The owner and bartender was Graham Ross, a true "character" who developed a "character" establishment which catered to a strange collection of modern day "hippies," recluses and assorted modern civilization misfits who found a sort of Nirvana in the junk kept hills of Silver City a few years ago. Authority was lax, living was simple (and cheap) and they all centered on the Golden Gate (partly because there wasn't much else). This liquor emporium was also the headquarters of the Silver City Fire Brigade, a self appointed rowdy bunch if there ever was one and quite proud of it as well. They particularly enjoyed disporting in various parades (Nevada Day, for instance) in nearby Carson City, always in totally dissolute and drunken array, making desultory and feeble attempts to play some improvised band instruments, and having one helluva good time. Certainly a better time than say – 95% of the spectators. This bar was begun in the 1930's and the name reportedly came from a sign someone found in a Reno junk yard.[4]

---

4) The Golden Gate Bar has a long and interesting history. It originally was an old Comstock era building, but was considerably run down until 1946 when a half interest was sold to Pat Staab. Pat was apparently a real character who made a go of it during the difficult late 40's and 50's by resorting to a multitude of tricks–such as installing a homemade horse inside the bar, tying a burro outside and placing a stuffed man on a rocking horse on the porch, all intended to attract customers. He also installed a loudspeaker on the roof so that he could "yell" at the tourists. Pat was a boomer though; he revitalized the Silver City Fire Department and was a main thrust in all local affairs. During the 1960's the "hippies discovered Silver City, but they proved good for business and the saloon prospered. In September, 1973 he sold the bar to Graham Ross (a sort of hippie himself) and retired to Missouri.

~ 127 ~

Frenchman Station in the center of Frenchman's Flat in Churchill County on the driest stretch of U. S. Highway 50 between Fallon and Austin was an interesting place and favorite "beer stop", until the U. S. Navy purchased the place (through threat of condemnation) and demolished it in the interests of National defense".

Frenchmen's Station about 1910. Photo: By Jerry Mock.

Pioneer Saloon: In Goodsprings, an old mining camp 34 miles southwest of Las Vegas. Built in 1913, it features a large cherrywood bar and back bar built in the 1860's. There is also an antique pot bellied stove and numerous (authentic) bullet holes in the walls and ceiling.

The Backstop Bar: In Boulder City exists in a nondescript storefront. There is an ornate mahogany back bar built in 1904 which was originally in a Los Angeles saloon. Now there is a bank of T.V. screens blaring forth sports events at all house, day and night.

The Exchange: Bill's place in Halleck (Elko County) obtained a bit of fame over the years. The original simple structure witnessing eight or nine murders before 1915. It operated as a local area saloon, somewhat more steadily from 1916 to 1970 when it was abandoned. This fine old bar and back bar is now on display at the Northwest Nevada Museum in Elko, where once a year it still serves it's original purpose.[5]

---

5) Once a year the Trustees of the Museum are required to gather around the bar for an anniversary drink. This was the sole "condition" attached to the gift of the bar to the museum some years ago.

TWENTY EIGHT

A SAMPLING OF SALOON MURDERS

Liquor related murder, both in saloons as well as frequently "out front" of one or more establishments, was quite commonplace in earlier Nevada. This was due to a number of factors including the very profusion of such places in the early communities, the fact that they were usually the "centers of action," the highly armed state of the patrons, the often basic depravity of the contestants, and of course the frequently inebriated state of the various players. Be that as it may, a lot of mayhem took place which is directly connectable to the saloons together with their related gambling and sometimes girls (upstairs).

There were many such murders, far too many to detail. Following are a sampling of a few, all quite typical of the time:

The little community of Bristol, some 22 miles northwesterly from Pioche in Lincoln County, is only a spot on an old map today, but during the period from 1871 to 1884, it , as many others, exhibited a boom character and the usual lawlessness associated with the Pioche area. Mormons discovered silver here in 1870, resulting in the camp named National City. Activity was slow until 1878 when a 12 stamp mill was erected and the camp renamed Bristol. By 1882 the town had five stores, two hotels (with restaurants attached), three stables, a lodging house, express office, two barber shops as well as eight saloons, with plenty of whiskey. It was in one of the ubiquitous saloons on a cold evening in January that A. K. Lesher, a well known local blacksmith, met William Thomas, a teamster. The two had been bickering and threatening each other for about a week, loudly quarreling whenever they met, and usually requiring bystanders to interfere in order to prevent outright hostility. It was apparent to all that "bad blood" existed between the two, although no one really knew the cause of it. After a few words which grew increasingly acrimonious, Thomas, a large and somewhat beefy man, requested Lesher to "go out into the street with him and fight a fair battle without other than natural resources and thus settle all our difficulties." Lesher was not too enthusiastic about this and refused to fight Thomas in that manner. Thomas then left the saloon loudly indicating his intent to return ready to fight with a pistol. Lesher remained at the table and in a few minutes Thomas did return with a gun. Upon his entry Lesher rose from his sitting position firing the first shot as he did so, but without effect. The two men stood face to face within three feet of each other, each with an arm extended and their pistols aimed. Both fired "instanter" and Thomas fell to the floor shot through the heart. Lesher was unhurt, a miraculous delivery duly explained by the fact that the ball from Thomas' pistol had gone barely beyond the muzzle and dropped to the floor as a result of a defective cartridge. Lesher was arrested immediately, but after an examination before the Justice of the Peace, was discharged on the ground that the killing was justifiable.

Aurora, in Esmeralda County, high in the mountains, close to the California State Line, was a particularly unhealthy place. All mining camps in the 1860's were "tough" and there was little scarcity of murder and mayhem, but "a man for breakfast" became so commonplace in Aurora between 1861 and 1863 that a sort of callousness pervaded the community and people even stopped bothering to ask for details. From almost the beginning of the town, it was invaded by two rival gangs of "toughs." One of these came from Sacramento; the other from the seamier side of San Francisco. These groups were constantly drinking and fighting and the resultant mortality rate was enormous: About half of these murders were rival gang members; the remainder were innocent bystanders. During the early years of the 1860's there were 27 confirmed murders (plus innumerable lesser affairs) but not one single conviction. In the spring of 1864 it went too far. It started with a single case of horse thievery. A Jimmy Sears (or Sayers) stole Louis Wedertz's favorite horse. Wedertz followed the trail to Wellington Station where he appealed to the agent in charge, a W. R. Johnson, for help. Johnson sent a man to continue the pursuit; he performed admirably, shortly returning with the horse, but leaving a corpse near Sweetwater. Sears' cronies reacted, although not against either Wedertz or Rogers (the man who retrieved the horse). They decided instead to get Johnson, a symbol in their minds of good clean conduct and stability, which was an anathema to them. They lured him to Aurora (presumably to discuss an interest in a stage station at Adobe Meadows,[1] and then spent the evening hours at one of the many Aurora saloons. About 4:30 A.M., Johnson retired to his hotel, but on the way was shot down on Antelope Street near the very center of town. In order to further enforce their attitude, the gang then cut Johnson's throat and set fire to his clothes. Immediately upon hearing the news that morning, a vigilante committee was formed. Within hours, every known tough, to their immense surprise, was taken to jail where extra guards were conspicuously on duty. Sheriff Francis and a posse were also combing the hills for Wm. Buckly, known to be in on the murder, but who had prudently fled the town. Deputy Teel was "arrested" and placed under guard in his own home so that he could not interfere. Francis soon returned with Buckly, and he too joined the group under guard. Singled out as the gang leaders who were mainly responsible for Johnson's death were Buckly, John Dailey, James Masterson and John (3 fingered Jack) McDowell. The vigilantes, now known as the "Citizen's Safety Committee," held a preliminary hearing for these four, as well as some others, at the old police station. One of Dailey's men by the name of Vance, began some trouble and was quickly shot—then carted off to jail. The Safety Committee, some 350 strong, setup court in Armory Hall.

The accused were given fair trials, the juries functioned as they should and the court decided that Dailey, Masterson, McDowell and Buckly should hang and that Irish Tom Canberry should leave town forever immediately. These trials were underway for eight days, during which time no liquor was served after 9:00 P.M. The streets were notable for their quiet and no sound of gunfire was heard, a record in itself. On the morning of the ninth day, the news reached Governor Nye, in Carson City, who telegraphed immediately requesting that there be no violence. A return message indicated to the good Governor that the situation was "all quiet and orderly; four men will hang in half an hour." At noon that day the four were hung—all at once and together. Immediately afterwards the remaining town toughs were released and advised to leave instantly, which they did. From then on, Aurora was a peaceful, steady town, although as some complained, "somewhat dull at times."

---

1)   Adobe Meadows was an isolated way station some 40 miles southerly of Aurora. It was known as a rough place. One winter night in 1863 a group of local toughs were drinking when the door opened to reveal a horseman. He was cordially invited to dismount and come inside, but the rider indicated he was too cold and stiff and would need some help. This incited some sympathy and the genial host resolved the situation by drawing his pistol and shooting the horse. The rider was told, "Now you can get off all right."

One night a poor wretch named McGuire, who picked up a slim and nefarious living hanging around the various gambling houses, went to sleep on a unused billiard table in the rear of one of the many saloons which graced the main street of Aurora. A local tough, one Johnson Donovan, came in, and seeing the sleeping man, calmly drew his knife and stabbed him—to the hilt—apparently for no reason. Even the "rougher" elements of the community did not consider it "right" to stab a sleeping man, so Donovan was arrested and taken to the Justice of the Peace. There, after some frontier type of rationale, it was determined that McGuire was a "worthless, no account cus, anyway." The facts of the case were totally disregarded and Donovan was duly freed; the case was considered "justifiable homicide."

On another (normal) night in Aurora, a man leaving one of the many saloons was shot and robbed near a gulch filled with slime from the Westside Mill. The body lay in the street for some time until the millers became worried and thought it best to dispose of the evidence. They then threw it into the slime pool where it sank and was conveniently lost. It was positively known that a householder within fifty feet of the place of the crime had opened his window and talked to the killers, but at the delayed hearing he testified under oath that he had heard no shot, seen no one, and knew nothing. This ended the matter and nothing further was done.

In Aurora, another killing was that of Bill Gardner by Mose Brockman. It was a necessity, more or less. Gardner was a crack shot—said he could push his hat off the back of his head, draw and put a bullet through it before it hit the ground. Mose had been warned repeatedly that he had to face this man or be killed on sight. He decided to take no chance and watching Gardner's movements, he saw him enter a saloon in the Novacovich Building. He then hid himself in a doorway and when Gardner appeared, gave him both barrels of buckshot, ending Gardner's career quite quickly, and quite efficiently.

Again, in Aurora, a Frank Shaw somehow aroused the anger of another man named Carter, who sent word to Shaw that he intended to kill him on sight. Shaw, taking no chances, as Carter came through the door of the saloon, shot and killed him with a shotgun. But Carter had seen Shaw and also drew and shot, but his bullet was slightly wide and struck a brick wall by Shaw's head, causing a splinter of brick to put out one of Shaw's eyes. After the trial at Aurora, (which strangely was held under California law even though the town is in Nevada), Shaw was acquitted, purchased a glass eye, and left the country.

On February 5, 1869, a Daniel Flynn, known as "Brocky", was killed by Pat Kelly (alias Pat Burns) in a quarrel at the Mammoth Saloon in Treasure City in White Pine County. Pat was going down some stairs, and instead of raising his arms as Davis commanded, he let them fall and Davis shot him with a shotgun. Davis fled, but was recaptured and escaped lynching by being taken to another place and strongly guarded. "The killing was most cowardly," was the only comment.

A young man, John Stewart, aged 24, killed a man in a Columbus saloon (in Esmeralda County) and was brought to Aurora to be tried. At the hearing it came out that he had killed two others before this latest event; he was duly convicted and sentenced to be hanged. When the day came, the officers asked if he had a last request. He did, one, that he be allowed the free indulgence of liquor from the time of leaving his cell to the platform. This request was granted and a local citizen was appointed as "bottle holder" to stand beside him and provide a drink whenever he desired it. Thus inspired, his last words were "If you take the mountain road, you will be murdered by Indians; if you take the trail, you will find no water and die of thirst. I must take the trail and in fifteen minutes, will be choked to death." In fifteen minutes that exact same thing happened (this was a rare case).

Pat Carrol was an exceptionally earnest Irish patriot and as preparations were being made for the 4th of July celebration, the miner's union of which Pat was a member, was invited to join the parade. Pat objected on the grounds that the U. S. had not done what it should for Ireland. He made so much trouble at the Miners Union Hall it took five men to eject him. He fortified himself at the nearest saloon and then returned. After a fierce scuffle, he drew the gun and fired one shot. The Committee replied in kind; Pat was outvoted and his funeral was held the next day!

Two bad men from Bodie, Led Ryan and Dave Bannon, got into a violent argument one day in back of one of the local thirst parlors. Each grabbed the other around the neck and began firing point blank against the other's body. Both were shot through and through.

In August 1868 Charles W. Humphries shot and killed W. Merritt in Wadsworth. From testimony presented before Justice Bowker, it seems that McDermott was on a drunken spree, made some threats against the life of Humphries, and going into the saloon where Humphries was bartender, walked up to the bar and said, "You are pretty and I would just as soon kill you as any son of a bitch I know!" At the same time he drew a revolver from his belt. Humphries seized a gun from under the bar (kept there for that express purpose) and shot him dead. "Justice Bowker, very properly, we think, discharged the defendant and the verdict of the public is that Merritt was served just right," was the editorial comment.

One day a miner came to a small isolated town from the nearby diggings and after a few belts at the bar sat in a game of cribbage at the table in back. His opponent was a well known professional gambler and it was not long before he began to cheat. The miner seeing this, swung the heavy handmade cribbage board, smashing the gambler's skull. Eyewitnesses testified "it was a natural death"—therefore, it was no crime. The jury agreed, the verdict was "not guilty, it served him right."

Rockland, a small and inconspicuous camp in the Pine Grove District in the Smith Valley Range, in southern Lyon County, never amounted to much. The camp was high in the mountains with a steep and dangerous trail leading down some 1,000 feet to Pine Grove, also a relatively inconsequential diggings. Recreation in these outlying areas was scarce. The mostly young and vigorous miners often had to improvise their own. And some times these affairs got out of hand. This occurred one spring payday night in 1872 when an impromptu "party" at the town's only saloon turned first into a spree and then into a free for all, all of which was instigated by a huge local, called, for want of greater detail, simply "Australian Kelly." The melee was a grand and glorious affair; everyone in camp soon joined in; some to prolong the affair for as long as possible, others to try to stop it. The only people in camp not involved were a few cripples, three Chinese cooks, and several other citizens who really wanted to join the fray, but were physically incapable of doing so. And, the bartender! The barkeep usually avoided fights such as these, if he could, since his primary allegiance was to protect his precious stock. This he did quite effectively with a large club stored behind the bar specifically for this purpose. The biting, kicking, wrestling, gouging and slugging was in full swing when someone put a knife into Kelly and ruined everything. This act sobered up the crowd immediately and Kelly's friends spread out to find the perpetrator, a John Crosser, named by Kelly in his last words. The constable found this person peacefully asleep in his bed, but he hauled him down without any gentleness to the combination jail and court room. Kelly's friends, still under the influence, decided that justice, at least quick justice, was unlikely, and decided to "get" Crosser themselves. They sent their biggest member, heavily armed, to do the job. As they entered the jail they found the constable and the Justice of the Peace questioning the totally bewildered (and still somewhat sleepy) Crosser. The appointed gunman shouted "You shall die" at Crosser, pulled out his revolver and aimed it at the confused prisoner. The usually mild tempered and peace loving J. P. was not about to see this type of justice prevail. This small, meek man instantly reacted, seized the big gunman, whirled him around and threw him bodily out the door. The gunman was so surprised at all of this he did not fire. The other members of the self appointed lynch mob stood open mouthed, but collected their bravado and made a rush for the prisoner only to find themselves staring down the muzzle of the constable's shotgun. The next day, a more complete investigation exonerated Crosser completely. Meanwhile, against all odds, Australian Kelly managed a complete recovery. The actual perpetrator was never discovered and peace returned to Rockland, at least for awhile.

In Virginia City, on the night of July 2, 1876, J. W. Fagan was killed by Tom Kelly over a quarrel. It seems that some years ago in Salt Lake City Fagan had a valuable dog which suddenly was missed and was not seen since. Kelly, who had been in Salt Lake at the time, now possessed a dog which looked suspiciously like the missing animal. Apparently Kelly was quite proud of his dog and claimed to have bought him. Fagan asserted that the dog was his and that he intended to take him. Both had keen drinking and quarreling all afternoon and evening—at more than passing vehemence—in the International Hotel. High words fully led to blows. Fagan slapped Kelly's face while the latter drew his pistol and struck Fagan over the head, cutting a deep gash, knocking him to his knees. He then fired two shots—one in Fagan's groin, completely severing the femoral artery. Fagan was unarmed. He did not speak and gasped for air for about fifteen minutes, then died. Kelly was arrested by Undersheriff Kinkaid and lodged in the local jail. His friends immediately came to his assistance, but to no avail. The body of Fagan was taken by the undertaker for later inquest. Fagan had arrived by emigrant trail the day before and was headed for Salt Lake City. He was a shoemaker by trade and left a wife and two children in Salt Lake City.

And then there was the stabbing and shooting of another Kelly, a Wm. J. Kelly, in Austin in August, 1876. Kelly was a late night watchman. He and a woman, Adelia Davis, somehow became involved in an altercation on Cedar Street. In the process Kelly was stabbed in the head and Davis shot in the thigh. It all started at the racetrack when Davis and Mollie Cotton had a quarrel which ended in a rough and tumble fight—which Kelly separated. After the races were over all parties returned to town when a shot was heard on Cedar Street. The crowd rushed over, arriving at Ralph Woodward's Saloon to find Kelly on the floor in a pool of blood where he died in a few minutes from the cruel gash. The body was taken to the Fireman's Hall and examined by Dr. Huntsman. The woman claimed to have been shot by Kelly, stayed in the Saloon until after the examination when she was taken home. The *Reese River Reveille* found all this quite confusing and ended up by saying "this seems to be a very complicated case and we find it impossible to get the facts."

Rhyolite, about four miles southwest of Beatty, was discovered by the famous "Shorty" Harris (a single blanket jackass prospector) during the fall of 1904. News of the find spread quickly and despite the approaching winter many people, especially from Tonopah and Goldfield, rushed to the site. In February, 1905, the town site was platted with free lots offered to merchants. The town developed practically overnight; although at first limited to canvas, it soon developed with a more solid construction. During the remainder of 1905 and through 1906 many new fortune seekers arrived pushing property values to astronomic heights (for those days). Stock speculation paralleled the boom and wildcat companies flourished. By 1907 the community had over 6,000 population, boasting even an opera house and two locally printed magazines.

One of the many new citizens migrating from Tonopah and generally a good fellow, was a middle-aged miner named Steve O'Brien. He apparently was at one time President of the Tonopah Union Western Federation of Miners, but was not in good standing at this time. A typical Irish hard worker, he had "taken to drink" and when under the influence of liquor, which was plentiful and always available, became brutal and argumentative to the point his young wife of ten years was forced to leave him. The entire town soon knew of this condition. For awhile she supported herself and her eight year old daughter by nursing, but then she gradually developed a lodging house enterprise which was doing rather well since the area was filled with a large influx of men, all seeking their immediate fortune, and appropriate locations were scarce. Her (still) drunken husband continued to be a problem, however, and finally she decided to obtain a divorce, filing suit in the local court. He husband, learning of this action, went to see her at the Golden Hotel on the corner of Golden and Columbus Streets on a Friday, May afternoon in 1906, shortly after 2:00 P.M. to protest the pending separation. Following some argument, he became wild and unmanageable, shouting imprecations and swearing. He had with him a miner's candlestick, a forged metal device used to hold candles, the only source of light deep in the mines. These devices had a long 8" stem, sharpened at a point so that it could be jammed into the timbers . Before Mrs. O'Brien realized the danger, he seized her and thrust the impromptu "stiletto" into her heart. She ran from the hotel out into the street and collapsed. Several bystanders loaded her into a wagon to take her to the doctor. She died in his office in a nearby drug store. The shouting and excitement attracted Judge Donelly who attempted to disarm O' Brien (who had followed her into the street). However, O'Brien resisted and the struggle became quite fierce. Deputy Sheriff J. T. MacDonald now appeared and ordered O'Brien to desist and to "drop the weapon," but by now the miner was totally crazed and continued to belabor the Judge, inflicting several flesh wounds on the Judge with the same candlestick stiletto. The deputy, realizing the situation, then shot O'Brien killing him instantly. Several days later the Sheriff was exonerated. The local paper moralized at the end of the affair: "The fact that he was crazed with booze tells the whole story."

Even the State Capitol was not exempt. The following is an exact report of an item printed in the January 26, 1883, issue of *The Weekly Courier*:

MURDER AT CARSON

At Carson City, last Saturday morning at 2 o'clock, James Coombs, a gambler, shot and killed Jack Ross, one of the proprietors of the old Winston Saloon. It appears that Coombs had been losing very heavily at the gaming table during Friday, and therefore commenced drinking heavily, and on going into the Saloon, met Ross playing a game of cards, and asked him for the loan of $10, which was refused him, when he then in a fit of passion, struck Ross over the head with a cane. The two men then rushed out of the gambling room toward the bar, Ross being unarmed and endeavoring to either escape or reach a weapon.

As he reached the door leading into the saloon he received a ball in the side. After firing the shot Coombs slipped and fell and Ross, turning, sprang upon him and tried to wrench the pistol from his hand, when he received a second ball.

In regard to the critical part of the affray the *Carson Tribune* of last Saturday, says: "When Ross left the gambling room, Coombs followed, drawing his pistol, a 45 calibre English self-cocker. Before reaching the door leading from the gambling hall to the saloon, Ross' attention was attracted in some way, and turning, observed that Coombs had slipped and fallen to the floor. Seeing that he had a pistol leveled at him, Ross threw himself upon Coombs, endeavoring to wrest the weapon from the latter's hands, but Coombs, being a large and powerful man, retained his hold of the pistol and fired three shots at deceased. The first missed and lodged in the ceiling, the second entered the right side just above the hip, passing into the stomach; this caused Ross to relax his hold, and as he did Coombs murderously placed the muzzle of the weapon against the temple of the already fatally wounded man sending a ball crashing into his brain. Ross never spoke after receiving the wounds. Coombs made no effort to escape, and coming to the realization of the terrible deed he had committed, pleaded with the doctors to save the life of the prostrate man, remarking that he "had killed his best friend." Coombs was finally arrested and conveyed to the County Jail."

Deceased full name was John C. Ross. He was aged about thirty-one years, and was a native of Canada where he had a father, mother and sisters. He was for some years manager for Spooner & Company, and of late years has been in business in Carson.

Coombs is a man who weighs over 200 pounds. He is said to be good humored and pleasant when sober, but very abusive and quarrelsome when drunk.

Early Reno also had it share of saloon incited murders, most of which happened at one or two places along Virginia Street. The first occurred in April, 1869, when Henry Roth killed J. H. Miller by intent and one Henry Clay Phibbs, quite by accident. The act took place in the Reno Billiard Saloon, formerly Hammond's Saloon, recently acquired by two brothers, Henry Clay and John Quincy Phibbs, and located on the east side of Virginia Street not far from Commercial Row. It seems that Roth and Miller developed a dispute concerning some business interests in a nearby shoe shop, in which Roth was definitely the aggressor. Miller maintained his calm throughout until Roth, in a fit of temper, questioned Miller's ancestry. Miller shouted "You can't call me that," and immediately advanced towards Roth. Roth drew and cocked his revolver and as Phibbs was about to intervene, got Roth's' first bullet. Miller received the second one—in the back as he turned to flee. Constable Edwards, whose office was conveniently next door, was soon on the scene and disarmed Roth. Roth was subsequently sentenced to thirty-five years for killing Miller and eight years for doing away with Phibbs. One can't help but wonder at the discrepancy.

The Merchants Exchange Saloon, in Reno, was also the scene of several murders in the early years. The first took place on February 7, 1880, at 2:00 A.M. on Sunday morning. The Exchange, one of Reno's first booze dispensaries, stood on the west side of Virginia Street, just north of 2nd Street and was a popular gathering place. Two patrons, a man named Laswell, and one Barney Fitzgerald had squabbled over a card game the preceding day, wherein Laswell threatened to slap Fitzgerald's face if he caught him cheating again. This insult really bothered Fitzgerald, however, when later he met Laswell at the Exchange, asked to borrow money and was refused, he became really piqued. Fitzgerald retreated to one end of the long mahogany bar while Laswell took a similar position at the other end. Several shouted insults preceded the shooting. Laswell didn't get in a shot, but Fitzgerald hit him in the abdomen with the first shot, missed him with the second, and had his pistol misfire on the third. He then ran out in front, colliding with the town night watchman, a man named Ross. "Let me pass or I will blow your brains out", cried Fitzgerald. Ross was intelligent enough to let him pass and he soon disappeared into the night. Laswell, now in bad shape, was taken to the nearby home of some friends while the town police mounted a full scale hunt for Fitzgerald who hid out under a pile of gunnysacks in a remote cabin (the Sheriff found him thereby claiming the $100 reward he had himself offered for the capture). Near the hiding place, the officers found a woman's hat, two veils, and other feminine apparel which Fitzgerald "a small beardless youth", apparently intended to use as a disguise in his getaway. When notified that Fitzgerald had been captured Laswell exclaimed, "I am satisfied", and he died. Fitzgerald languished in the county jail for nine months before a jury found him guilty of Second Degree Murder and sentenced him to 12 years in prison.

The second affair in the Exchange Saloon took place in January of 1881, not quite a year later. James Mansel, more commonly known as "Poker Jim", and Frank Perkins, then one of the Exchange's co-owners, were engaged in a friendly game one Sunday evening when a dispute developed between them that broke up the game. Mansel (of course) was bounced from the premises. As he was forcible ejected, he threatened Perkins that "he would kill him." He finally purchased a revolver for eight dollars. He then continued to the Exchange Saloon to find Perkins tending bar. As he entered, Perkins told him quietly to leave. Mansel bounced out the door, but as he did, he drew his new gun muttering threats under his breath. Perkins saw the gesture and before Mansel could aim, Perkins grabbed his own pistol, and fired, hitting Mansel in the head. He fell to the floor immediately.

There were a number of witnesses to all this—and all agreed that Mansel intended to shoot Perkins "but was too slow." Perkins immediately gave himself up to the law where he was congratulated on his good aim and was released on a $2,000 bail. A jury later found him innocent.

A William Bacon, and old time prospector who had been a resident of the Willow Creek area near Osceola[2] in White Pine County for over 30 years, shot and seriously wounded a William Partridge on Sunday, July 1, 1917, near Willow Patch (Creek). Partridge was taken to the hospital where he died. It seems that both had been on a drunk in the nearest "thirst parlor" most of the night before and in the passage of time and drink had become involved in an altercation. Partridge wisely deciding to avoid further trouble, had returned to his house and was sitting in the door of his cabin when Bacon rode up and fired at him, apparently without provocation. Partridge later died, but nothing happened to Bacon, even though he had been in trouble with the law some ten years previously.

Sometimes, a particular saloon in a community tended to attract more than a fair share of one of these was the Gem Bar in Winnemucca, which had a long and bloody history, reflective of May 6, 1869, a shooting occurred there involving Tom Marker, and a party named "Boston" Parson. Five shots were fired in all unhurt, delivered himself to the Sheriff, and following a hearing, he was discharged. Hopes were held for the recovery of Boston, but it was not reported whether he made it or not. In September, 1876, another killing occurred there when James Hubler was shot by Led Gillis. Gillis was sentenced to 15 years in the State Prison for Second Degree Murder. Not quite a year later, on the 4th of July, 1877, Charley Harris and James Randall, a Civil War Veteran, both employees of the Northwestern Stage Company, were frequent patrons at the bar. A dispute over a debt one owed the other ended on the sidewalk when Randall died from a shot to the head. Harris was also sent to prison for 18 years. In October, 1890, Dick Lewis shot and killed A. H. Ruse, a mining man, due to presumed derogatory remarks at the bar. Lewis was later found to be insane. In 1922, (August) bad blood existed between a man named John Harris and Claude Silvers, the bartender. Silvers died behind his bar from a gunshot by Harris, who also then visited the State Prison.

On Christmas night 1862, R. T. (Butcher) Ferris killed W. Brown at a dance in the Pioneer Hotel in Unionville. He was never tried for this act.

---

2) Osceola was organized in 1872, as a placer mining area and was the first operation in Nevada utilizing hydraulic hoses. A post office was started in 1878, closing in 1924.

The number of murders and mayhem associated with the Nevada Saloon did not slow down at the turn of the century, or even after the 1906 boom that resulted in so many later towns, but was continued, even to this day, although in much lesser proportions due to many "changes in circumstances."

Quite often saloon related murders were for little or no reason. Often the combatants did not even know each other. Liquor made tempers easily aroused, inflamed egos created an atmosphere of supposed affronts, even when of the most minor nature, which demanded instant and total response. A perfect example of this is detailed in the following account:

The Town of Bullfrog in southern Nye County, together wit its sister camp of Rhyolite, were some four miles west of the little town of Beatty, and both were usually rather quiet. Bullfrog was really a later camp in Nevada mining history, beginning after the main excitement in the fall of 1904. It grew rapidly, however, and after only several years listed over 1,000 residents, with the usual number of saloons, a post office, several hotels, a band and even a Chamber of Commerce. Bullfrog adjoined the town of Rhyolite and by 1906 most of the commercial activities had moved to this more active and larger camp, although many fine residences and post office remained in Bullfrog.

By May 1905, only eight months from inception, the town was thriving. The short main street was lined with ten businesses, new people were arriving daily and fast auto stages were shuttling regularly to nearby Beatty as well as to Rhyolite and Gold Center. That summer was a "boomer" as many new miners, fortune seekers and others flooded the new camp.

On Friday evening of October 13, Durkee's Saloon was jammed with some of these new arrivals. The long bar was well used, the poker table was equally active and A. J. Jodoin, a stone mason, was well ahead of the game. Jodoin was 33 years old, from Rhode Island and had arrived in the town in December, 1904. An onlooker, a huge man named Bob Arnold, asked if he was playing. Jodoin offhandedly said, "I have carried more money than any of you fellows." Arnold asked, "Do you include me?" "Yes, you as well as anyone," replied Jodoin. Arnold then pulled his revolver and beat Jodoin over the head with it causing a bloody gash and knocking him to the floor. Jodoin struggled to his feet to continue the fight, but realizing he was unarmed, thought better of it and fled out on the main street going to a water trough to wash the blood off. He then went home.

The following morning Jodoin appeared at Durkee's but no one was there so he went to Rhyolite to have his wounds treated. Returning to Bullfrog he entered Wandell's Saloon, again meeting Arnold, although accidently, and the quarrel resumed immediately. Jodoin backed toward the door, starting to remove his coat and dared Arnold to step outside and fight it out with their fists. Arnold refused to "step outside." Jodoin the shouted, "You big cur, you're not man enough." Arnold reached for his gun; the crowded room cleared as if by magic. Jodoin had also snatched his gun ()as he was armed this time) but before he could draw, Arnold fired, but missed. Jodoin took hasty aim through the gun smoke and fired, hitting Arnold in the abdomen, but the big man did not fall. Staggered he leaned on the poker table, raised his gun and again emptied it in the direction of Jodoin. Miraculously, Jodoin wasn't hit in this fusillade, but was so rattled that his next three return shots missed Arnold as he finally slumped to the floor. Arnold was "laid out" upon a nearby billiard table where he died some 35 minutes later.

Jodoin was held for trial before Judge Morris with Assistant District Attorney Thomas prosecuting. Messr. Davis and Arnold (no relation), two young attorneys who just happened to step off the stage as the shooting was taking place, obtained their first case "instanter" in the handling of a defense. After a four day examination a coroner's jury brought in a verdict of "self defense," at which point the attorneys on both sides congratulated Jodoin. Jodoin was released, never to be heard from again.

A typical pioneer saloon, now long abandoned. This one happens to be the <u>Palace</u> in Golconda, but it could have looked almost the same in any number of rural spots. "Palace" was a very popular name for Nevada saloons; they are found in many camps. Compare this one to the <u>Palace</u> in Winnemucca.
There was a <u>Palace Club</u> in Goldfield, and also one in Reno. Photo: By the author.

TWENTY NINE

OVERVIEW AND RATING SYSTEM

In order to measure the relative integrity of modern day bars against the character and style of their earlier counterparts, some criteria must be established. After considerable exposure to a large number of present day saloons, and a close scrutiny of pictures of more ancient ones, the following basic points of consideration become paramount. They are, of course very subjective and the relative "weighting" of each against the others, is totally up to the observer.

1. The saloon must be (primarily) a drinking bar -not an emporium for "T" shirts, gifts, hot dogs or a playground for children.

2. There must be a minimum of slot machines - and <u>none</u> inset into the bar itself.

3. There must be a minimum of plastic and neon, inside and out. (preferably none – somewhat difficult now days)

4. (Preferably) there should be no canned music or a constantly playing M.T.V. This includes juke boxes.

5. There must be an "old time character" in age, or decor or both. (This is most important, but admittedly is the most difficult to value).

6. The establishment must be open consistently—not just on weekends or during hunting season.

7. There should be a "friendly" (and knowledgeable) bartender.

8. The saloon must function as a social center for a local area.

9. Limited gaming, pool tables and a small dance floor may be acceptable under certain conditions.

10. It must definitely not be (consciously) a tourist trap.

With these points in mind, but only as general guidelines, please feel free to draw your own list … and your own conclusions.

ABOUT THE AUTHOR

This is the second book by Raymond M. Smith, now living in Minden, Nevada. He was born and raised in San Francisco. He attended Stanford University before enlisting in 1942, returning there in 1945, after discharge from Air Force, having been in active combat in Italy. He graduated from Stanford in Architectural Design in 1947 and then was awarded a Master Degree in City and Regional Planning from the Graduate School of Design at Harvard University in 1949. He came to Reno that year as the Director of Regional Planning Commission of Reno, Sparks and Washoe County (ten years), the Vice President of the Crystal Bay Development Company at Incline Village (three years), and a private consultant throughout Northern Nevada for over 30 years. He is also a recognized historian and lecturer, as well as a court expert concerning land and development matters, and is a watercolor painter of ghost towns, old buildings and Nevada landscapes.

He has been married to a Dutch-born lady for 46 years and has four grown native sons, all still living in Nevada.

For the last 45 years he has been an avid outdoorsman, hunter, explorer and artist of the rural and primitive Nevada scene. Mr. Smith has lived in Reno, Lake Tahoe, and Carson Valley, but has travelled extensively throughout the northern portion of the state. This has resulted in a deep understanding of the physical, social and economic parameters which have shaped the history and character of the area.

His first book, entitled "Untold Tales of Carson, Eagle and Smith Valleys" (Vol. I) was published in late 1991. It details a number of true, but little known people, places and events of the region which "cannot be found in history books."

His third book released in 1992 entitled "Travels in the Nevada Outback," recounts a number of desert places and person encountered in wandering the playas and canyons of central Nevada. The fourth book (1994) is a continuation of Volume I of "Untold Tales,' while the fifth book is a sort of travel log describing ten overnight trips on the back roads of Western Nevada and the California Sierra. A new book; "Nevada's Northwest Corner" details the still relatively unknown Black Rock country of northern Washoe and Humboldt Counties. It is due for publication in the summer of 1996.